HISTORY OF THE FIRST WORLD WAR

'Immensely readable and informative ... belongs in the possession of anyone interested in what the greatest British military thinker of this century has to say ...' THE SOLDIER

'Liddell Hart makes the complicated scene intelligible to the reader with the minimum of effort, and yet incorporates an apt and telling comment at every turn' THE TIMES LITERARY SUPPLEMENT

'Remarkable for its clarity and objectivity, and for analysis undistorted by professional prejudice or by bitterness over the unrecallable past. It remains outstanding: for those familiar with its subject, illuminating and thought-provoking; for those new to it and wishing to know what happened in World War I, the best place to begin' WESTERN MAIL

One of the world's outstanding teacher-historians, Sir Basil Liddell Hart was born in Paris in 1895 and educated at St Paul's and Corpus Christi College, Cambridge. He joined the Army (King's Own Yorkshire Light Infantry) and served in the First World War; in 1924 he was invalided and three years later retired with the rank of Captain. He evolved several military tactical developments including the Battle Drill system and was an early advocate of airpower and armoured forces. In 1937 he became personal adviser to the War Minister, but reorganization of the Army was so slow that he resigned a year later to press the need publicly.

Liddell Hart was military correspondent to the *Daily Telegraph* from 1925–35 and to *The Times* until the outbreak of the Second World War. He lectured on strategy and tactics at staff colleges in numerous countries and wrote more than thirty books. He died in 1970.

Also by B. H. Liddell Hart in Papermac
History of the Second World War

B. H. Liddell Hart

HISTORY OF THE
FIRST WORLD WAR

PAPERMAC

First published 1930 as *The Real War, 1914-1918*
by Faber and Faber Ltd. Enlarged edition published 1934
as *A History of the World War 1914-1918*
Published 1970 as *History of the First World War*
by Cassell and Co Ltd

This edition published 1997 by Papermac
an imprint of Macmillan Publishers Ltd
25 Eccleston Place, London SW1W 9NF
Basingstoke and Oxford
Associated companies throughout the world
www.macmillan.co.uk

ISBN 0 330 58261 6

9 8

A CIP catalogue record for this book is available from
the British Library.

Printed and bound in Great Britain by
Mackays of Chatham PLC, Chatham, Kent

TO JOHN BROWN AND THE LEGION

ACKNOWLEDGEMENTS

I wish to acknowledge the kindness of those who read various parts of this book in proof, and their helpfulness in contributing criticisms and suggestions. They include Lieut-Colonel H. G. de Waterville, Mr E. G. Hawke, and one unnamed whose knowledge of sources was as boundless as the trouble he took to aid me.

Original Preface to
A History of The World War

It is more than four years since *The Real War* was published. That title was chosen for reasons explained above. It fulfilled a purpose, but with the passage of time the need for it has passed. As a summary of the significant facts of the war it has met no serious challenge, and even its interpretation of them has been endorsed by the innermost observers of events, in the various countries, to an extent which has come as a pleasant surprise to the author. Now, twenty years have passed since the war came, and a generation has grown up that has no personal memory of it. The war is history. Hence the time has come, as well as the justification, for adopting a title that has no longer a contemporary note. An enlargement of the contents is a further reason. However much it still falls short of completeness, and my own ideal, it may at least be termed 'a history' of the World War. Also it may contribute to the growth of *the* history of the World War.

It is itself a growth from *The Real War*, just as the original volume evolved from a series of monographs on particular aspects and episodes. Personal experience makes me doubt whether it would be possible to compile a satisfactory history of 1914–18 by a less gradual method. Confronted suddenly by a whole mass of evidence now at hand, it would be difficult to maintain a clear view, and so easy for the pattern to be distorted by the very weight of the records. For my own part, I have found the practical value of a method which has allowed me, over a period of years, to fit each fresh bit of evidence into an expanding frame.

In evolving the present volume from *The Real War* there has been some revision, but more enlargement. 'The Opposing Forces and Plans' are now described in separate chapters, each augmented by new material. Two new 'scenes' have been added to make the story of 1914 more complete: one deals with the opening clash of the Austrian and Russian armies; and the other with the autumn struggle at Ypres and on the Yser which determined the possession of the Channel ports. An outline of the war in the air is given under the title 'Panorama'. But the greater part of the enlargement is due to the expansion of the existing chapters and 'scenes' through the incorporation of fresh evidence that has come to attention on the thoughts and feelings of some of the pawns of war. The war was, it is true, waged and decided in the minds of individuals more than in the physical clash of forces. But these decisive impressions were received and made in the cabinets and in the military headquarters, not in the ranks of the infantry or in the solitude of stricken homes.

The other – and more intentional – meaning of the title is that the time has come when a 'real' history of the war is possible. Governments have opened their archives, statesmen and generals their hearts with an unparalleled philanthropy. It is safe to say that most of the possible documentary evidence on the war has now been published or is available for the student. But it has not yet been collated for the information of the public.

The flood of documents, diaries and memoirs has one outstanding advantage. They have come when they can still be tested by the personal witness of those who took part in the crises and critical discussions of the war. A few years hence would be too late. Yet in the application of this test lies the only chance that history may approximate to truth. The more that any writer of history has himself been at hand when history is being made, or in contact with the makers, the more does he come to see that a history based solely on formal documents is essentially superficial. Too often, also, it is the unwitting handmaiden of 'mythology'.

Original Preface to
The Real War

On finishing this book I am conscious of its imperfections – some consolation comes from the reflection that every book worth reading is imperfect. This book may at least claim one merit, and one contrast to most war 'histories'. I have as little desire to hide its imperfections as to hide the imperfections of any who are portrayed in its pages. Hence in writing it my pursuit of the truth has not been interrupted by recourse to the pot of hypocritical varnish that is miscalled 'good taste'. In my judgement of values it is more important to provide material for a true verdict than to gloss over disturbing facts so that individual reputations may be preserved at the price of another holocaust of lives. Taking a long view of history, I cannot regard the repute of a few embodied handfuls of dust as worth more than the fate of a nation and a generation.

On the other hand, I have equally little desire to exaggerate the imperfections of individuals for the sake of a popular effect, or to shift on to them the weight of folly and error which should be borne by the people as a whole.

The historian's rightful task is to distil experience as a medicinal warning for future generations, not to distil a drug. Having fulfilled this task to the best of his ability, and honesty, he has fulfilled his purpose. He would be a rash optimist if he believed that the next generation would trouble to absorb the warning. History at least teaches the historian a lesson.

The title of this book, which has a duality of meaning, requires a brief explanation. Some may say that the war depicted here is not 'the real war' – that this is to be discovered in the torn bodies and minds of individuals. It is far from my purpose to ignore or deny this aspect of the truth. But for anyone who seeks, as I seek here, to view the war as an episode in human history, it is a secondary aspect. Because the war affected individual lives so greatly, because these individuals were numbered by millions, because the roots of their fate lay so deep in the past, it is all the more necessary to see the war in perspective, and to disentangle its main threads from the accidents of human misery. Perhaps this attempt is all the more desirable by reason of the trend of recent war literature, which is not merely individualistic but focuses light in the past four years. Thus, in the chapter outlines, there is somewhat fuller treatment of the German advance into France in 1914; the Austro-German offensive against Russia and the Balkan situation in 1915; the Palestine situation in 1916; the spring campaign of 1917 on the Western Front; and the Allied discussions which preceded the German offensives of 1918. The main expansion, however, and most of the new material, will be found in the 'scenes', especially those which deal with Verdun, the Somme, Passchendaele, the 'First Breakthrough' and the 'Breakthrough in Flanders'. To a lesser extent, there is an infusion of fresh facts about the Brusilov, the Arras, the Messines and the Cambrai offensives, and the Second Battle of the Marne.

The revision needed has been comparatively slight. But new evidence that has come out in the past four years has led me to modify my view of such questions as the German strategy at Verdun, the projected move against Austria, the cause of Nivelle's failure in 1917, the Versailles committee and the preparations to meet the German offensive in 1918. On a number of points, fuller knowledge has amplified the earlier view, and while it has tended to illuminate the mistakes that were committed, it has also helped to elucidate their cause. I have also modified or omitted my original comments on certain episodes, and in their place have quoted from the evidence of those who were responsible, leaving the facts to form the conclusion.

CONTENTS

Chapter One
THE ORIGINS OF THE WAR
1

Chapter Two
THE OPPOSING FORCES
28

Chapter Three
THE RIVAL WAR PLANS
40

Chapter Four
THE CLINCH
(1914)
49

Scene 1	The Marne	78
Scene 2	Tannenberg	97
Scene 3	Lemberg	107
Scene 4	'First Ypres'	118

Chapter Five
THE DEADLOCK
(1915)
132

Scene 1	The Dardanelles	157
Scene 2	The Landing on Gallipoli	170
Scene 3	'Second Ypres'	183
Scene 4	Loos	193

CONTENTS

Chapter Six
THE 'DOG-FALL'
(1916)
204

Scene 1	Verdun	217
Scene 2	The Brusilov Offensive	227
Scene 3	The Somme	231
Scene 4	The Tank	254
Scene 5	Rumania	263
Scene 6	Baghdad	269
Scene 7	Jutland	274

Chapter Seven
THE STRAIN
(1917)
295

Scene 1	Arras	314
Scene 2	Messines	322
Scene 3	Passchendaele	327
Scene 4	Cambrai	337
Scene 5	Caporetto	349
Panorama: The War in the Air		355

Chapter Eight
THE BREAK
(1918)
362

Scene 1	The First Breakthrough	384
Scene 2	The Breakthrough in Flanders	399
Scene 3	The Breakthrough to the Marne	407
Scene 4	The Second Battle of the Marne, July, 1918	415
Scene 5	'August 8th'	423
Scene 6	Megiddo	432
Scene 7	St Mihiel	441
Scene 8	The Meuse-Argonne	451

CONTENTS

EPILOGUE
459

BIBLIOGRAPHY
465

INDEX
491

MAPS

drawn by Peter McClure

The Western Front	50
The Eastern Front	66
The Marne – 1914	79
Tannenberg – 1914	98
Lemberg – 1914	108
Gallipoli	171
Ypres – 1915	184
Loos – 1915	194
Verdun – 1916	218
Somme – 1916	230
Rumania	264
Mesopotamia	270
Jutland	275
Jutland	293
Arras – April, 1917	315
Ypres – 1917	328
Cambrai – 1917	338
Caporetto	350
German Offensive – March, 1918	382
The Lys – April, 1918	400
The Breakthrough to the Marne	408
Second Battle of the Marne	414
Amiens – August 8th, 1918	424
Megiddo – 1918	433
St Mihiel	442
Meuse-Argonne	452

CHAPTER ONE

The Origins of the War

Fifty years were spent in the process of making Europe explosive. Five days were enough to detonate it. To study the manufacture of the explosive materials – which form the fundamental causes of the conflict – is within neither the scope nor the space of a short history of the World War. On the one side we should have to trace the influence of Prussia on the creation of the Reich, the political conceptions of Bismarck, the philosophical tendencies in Germany, and the economic situation – a medley of factors which transmuted Germany's natural desire for commercial outlets, unhappily difficult to obtain, into a vision of world power. We should have to analyse that heterogeneous relic of the Middle Ages known as Austria-Hungary, appreciate her complex racial problems, the artificiality of her governing institutions, the superficial ambitions which overlay a haunting fear of internal disruption and frantically sought to postpone the inevitable end.

On the other side we should have to examine the strange mixture of ambition and idealism which swayed Russia's policy, and the fear it generated beyond her frontiers, especially among her German neighbours – perhaps the deadliest of all the ingredients in the final detonation. We should have to understand the constant alarms of fresh aggression which France had suffered since 1870, study the regrowth of confidence which fortified her to resist further threats, and bear in mind the wounds left in her side by Germany's surgical excision of Alsace-Lorraine. Finally, we should have to trace Britain's gradual movement from a policy of isolation into membership of the European system and her slow awakening to the reality of German feeling towards her.

In such a study of European history during half a century, a generalization can for once be closer to exactness than the most detailed history. The fundamental causes of the conflict can be epitomized in three words – fear, hunger, pride. Beside them, the international 'incidents' that occurred between 1871 and 1914 are but symptoms.

All that is possible, and sensible, here is to trace the most significant turning points in the trail of causation which led to combustion. This trail runs through the structure of alliances which Bismarck built after 1871. Ironically, Bismarck intended it as a shelter for the peaceful growth of his creation, the German Empire, and not as a magazine for explosives. For although his philosophy was epitomized in his 1868 phrase – 'The weak were made to be devoured by the strong' – his own hunger was satiated, after three meals, by the war of 1870–71. It cannot be charged against him that his eyes were larger than his stomach; feeling that Germany now was, as he said, a 'saturated' state, his governing idea henceforth was not expansion but consolidation. And to secure time and peace for this consolidation of the new Germany he aimed to keep France in a state of permanent powerlessness to wage a war of revenge. But the result was to prove that two wrongs do not make a Reich.

Apart from frequent direct menaces to France, he sought to counteract her annoyingly rapid recovery by the indirect method of depriving her of friends or supporters. To this end his first effort was to bring Austria and Russia together by forging a common link with Germany, while he strove to ensure peace in the Balkans as a means to avoid any dangerous strain on the link. For some years his policy was that of acting as the 'honest broker' in the diplomatic exchange of Europe without committing himself to any party. But friction with the Russian chancellor, Gortchakov, and the complications caused by the Russo-Turkish war of 1877, led him to make a defensive alliance with Austria in 1879, despite the objections of the old Emperor William I, who regarded it as 'treachery' to Russia and even threatened to abdicate. This definite commitment was to have infinite consequences. Nevertheless, Bismarck temporarily regained his central position by his diplomatic masterstroke of 1881, the famous 'three emperors' alliance', whereby Russia, Austria and Germany undertook to act together in all Balkan affairs. And although it lapsed in 1887, Germany's connexion with Russia was strengthened in compensation by the secret 'Reinsurance Treaty', by which the two powers agreed to maintain benevolent neutrality towards each other in case of war with a third. It was not, however, to apply if Germany attacked France or Russia attacked Austria. By this second masterstroke, executed with great duplicity, Bismarck averted the risk, then imminent, of an alliance between Russia and France.

Meantime, the alliance between Germany and Austria had been enlarged by the inclusion of Italy in 1882. The object was to safeguard Austria against a stab in the back if at war with Russia, and in return

Italy's new allies would come to her assistance if attacked by France. But as a safeguard to her old friendship with Britain and to her own coasts, Italy had a special protocol appended to the treaty stating that it was in no case to be directed against Britain. In 1883, Rumania, through her King's personal and secret act, was attached to the new Triple Alliance. Even Serbia was temporarily linked on by a separate treaty with Austria, and Spain by an agreement with Italy.

In regard to Britain, Bismarck's aim seems to have been to keep her in friendly isolation from Germany and unfriendly isolation from France. His feelings towards Britain oscillated between friendship and contempt, and the political party system formed the pivot. For the 'old Jew', Disraeli, he had genuine respect, but he could not understand the point of view of the Gladstonian Liberals, and their wavering actions he despised. While Disraeli was in power Bismarck toyed with the idea of linking Britain to his chain of alliances, but although Queen Victoria was plaintively 'sure that Germany would be the safest ally in every way', she was less sure of Bismarck's safety as a repository of trust, and Disraeli shared her doubts. Hence Bismarck continued, with equal satisfaction, his policy of playing off Britain against Russia and France in turn. And with shrewd calculation he favoured Britain's occupation of Egypt because it embroiled her with France, and resisted the growing clamour in Germany for colonial expansion – 'our colonial jingos' greed is greater than we need or can satisfy' – because it threatened future trouble with Britain, yet made his support to Britain in Egypt a means of extracting oversea concessions as morsels with which he could assuage the colonial hunger of a body of German interests too powerful even for him to ignore. The Conservatives' return to power in Britain, and the intensified friction with France, led to a fresh tightening of the links with Germany, and Bismarck's offer of a formal alliance was eagerly welcomed by Lord Salisbury's Cabinet who seem only to have held back from fear of Parliamentary objection to foreign entanglements. Bismarck, however, profited from the informal entente to secure the cession of Heligoland – so vital to German naval operations a generation later – at a paltry price.

Thus at the end of the eighties Bismarck's great structure seemed complete. Germany was buttressed by the Triple Alliance while the attached yet semi-detached position of Russia and Britain gave her advantages without encumbrances. From this secure base she was ready to develop her commercial expansion. And Bismarck had placed France in the combined solitude and circumscription of a political isolation ward.

But with the beginning of the nineties the first crack appeared in the structure, close upon the dismissal of the builder. The accession in 1888 of the young Emperor William II was disagreeable to the Tsar, Alexander III, who disliked his 'aggressive amiability' and distrusted his intentions. Yet the breach came not from Alexander, but from William. Bismarck's control irked him just as it irked the General Staff, and in the soldiers, among whom he had been brought up, he so naturally found allies that in linking himself with them he did not realize that he was forging fresh fetters for himself.

The first effect, after the dismissal of the 'pro-Russian' Chancellor, was his successor's refusal to renew the 'Reinsurance Treaty' with Russia. The second effect, a natural sequel to the first, was that the Tsar swallowed his aversion to republicanism and, in 1891, made an agreement with France which, a year later, was developed into a military convention for mutual assistance in case of attack. In this convention a significant point was that if any member of the Triple Alliance mobilized its forces, both France and Russia were instantly to mobilize. The Tsar at least could not complain that he did not understand the meaning, for the French negotiator, General Boisdeffre, took pains to explain that 'mobilization means declaration of war'.

In the Tsar's case, the draught was swallowed under the fear that Britain was about to ally herself with Germany; it lay heavy on his stomach, so that it was long in producing any diplomatic value for France.

Nevertheless, France had left 'quarantine'. Henceforth there was not one political group, but two, in Europe. Although one was loose, the other compact, the two groups formed a balance of power, if their power was not yet balanced evenly.

A doubly significant sidelight upon Germany's renunciation of the Russian secret treaty is that the council in Berlin which reviewed the matter decided against the treaty on the ground that it was disloyal not only to Austria but to Britain. Whatever the Kaiser's failings, he was more sincere than Bismarck, and the insincerity apparent in his contradictory utterances seems to have been due to his combination of excessive frankness with a quick-changing mind. An essential difference between the two men was that the one sought security through consistent dishonesty, and the other gained insecurity through spasmodic honesty. The consideration shown for Britain was in accord with the Kaiser's views. For, although he had reversed Bismarck's attitude towards Russia, he maintained Bismarck's policy of friendship towards Britain, perhaps owing to more sincere, and less political motives. The one personal source of cleavage lay in the mutual antipathy of the Kaiser and his uncle, the Prince of Wales – later King Edward VII. And, curiously, it was the Bismarck family who worked to widen this personal breach.

But this could not have developed into a national cleavage without greater causes being at work. More truly, it was one cause with sundry accretions. Its origin and its foundation lay in Germany's change of policy from internal to external expansion. The growth of her commerce and influence to a world-wide scale inevitably brought her interests and those of Britain into contact at many points. Under tactful or even Bismarckian guileful handling this contact might not have caused such friction as to strike sparks, for British statesmanship was peculiarly insensitive. The party most conscious of Britain's imperial estate happened to be the party most sympathetic to imperial Germany. But Bismarck had gone and tact did not fill his place. As so commonly happens with great men, his disciples forgot his principles and remembered only his method – the mailed fist. Yet the Kaiser himself could also exert charm, and through it succeeded not only in maintaining his popularity in England despite repeated irritation, but in gaining a strong hold on the new and weakly amiable Tsar Nicholas II. For a time he thereby acquired influence without obligation.

The first friction with Britain came over Turkey – a shadow cast on the future. A Liberal government was in power again in 1892, when, as Grey relates, 'suddenly there came a sort of ultimatum from Berlin, requiring us to cease competition' with Germans 'for railway concessions in Turkey'. And in the years that followed the Kaiser lost no opportunity to emphasize that the spreading web of German commerce had a sharp-fanged spider at its centre. In 1895 his intervention made it possible for Russia to deprive Japan of her spoils in the war with China. In 1896 came the next, and more serious, friction with Britain. Ironically, its source was an Englishman's too ardent admiration for Bismarckian imperialism. The Kaiser, unsoothed by Rhodes' equal admiration for himself, became more and more irritated by Rhodes' schemes of British expansion in South Africa, frustrating his own. After several sour complaints, and sweet encouragement of the Transvaal Boers, he found a tempting pretext in the Jameson raid into the Transvaal. At a council on January 3rd, 1896, he suggested that Germany should proclaim a protectorate over the Transvaal and send troops thither. When the Chancellor, Hohenlohe, objected 'that would be war with England', the Kaiser ingenuously replied, 'Yes, but only on land.' As a less drastic alternative the Kaiser was encouraged to send a congratulatory telegram to President Kruger, so worded as not only to be highly offensive to Britain, but to deny her suzerainty over the Transvaal.

Popular feeling boiled over in both countries, due in the one case to ill-suppressed jealousy and in the other to pained surprise at discovering a fresh rival in a traditional friend. Germans felt a natural chagrin that Britain, with already so many colonies, should be gaining more in the one part of the world where a late-comer might hope to stake a claim. Englishmen had made such a habit of colonization that they blandly assumed it could only fit John Bull's figure, and could not understand that anyone, save the traditional rivals, France and Russia, might be anxious. However unconsciously provoking in ordinary intercourse, this calm assurance was a sedative in a crisis, and it largely saved this one. Warlike measures were actually ordered by Germany, and she suggested to France and Russia a combination against Britain. But lack of response from these countries, the calmness of Lord Salisbury's government, and a sense of her own naval weakness, restrained Germany and averted the immediate danger to peace.

But a danger put off by lack of power is not a danger removed. From this moment dates the real growth of German naval ambition, expressed in the Kaiser's words of 1897 – 'the trident must be in our fist' – and in the Kaiser's action of summoning Admiral Tirpitz to manufacture the trident. The next year saw the first large naval programme. It also heard the Kaiser proclaim himself, during his visit to Damascus, the protector of all Mohammedans throughout the world – a direct provocation to Britain and France. And not only to them. For the Kaiser's undisguised assumption of the role of patron saint of Turkey was fatal to his accord with Russia. His shadow now obscured Russia's view of Constantinople, the goal of her dreams. Like the opponents whom Napoleon derided, the Kaiser failed in policy because he 'saw too many things at once', and forced the other powers, whom Bismarck had played off against each other, to see only one thing – the fist of Germany – wherever they looked. Nevertheless, the affront to Britain in South Africa was followed, in 1898, by the offer from Chamberlain of that very alliance which Bismarck had sought in vain. But it was now the turn of Germany to be suspicious of the offer. On the British side the offer was impelled by a new and uncomfortable consciousness of isolation and weakness, while based on the old consciousness of natural affinity with Germany. But it looked, as it was in part, a confession of weakness, and weakness was not a quality to appeal to the new Germany. And one of Bismarck's few legacies to his successors was the habit of underrating Britain's strength and overrating Russia's.

In Germany's repeated rejections of Chamberlain's proposals between 1898 and 1901, the dominant factor was a personal factor – the concealed figure of Holstein. This crabbed, suspicious and miserly official of the Foreign Office, who loved obscurity because its dimness enhanced his real power in the pursuit of 'real policy', who would not buy himself a new suit although he did not shrink from using his official knowledge for private speculation, who had intrigued for his master's dismissal while posing as his pupil, was now viewed with awe as the spiritual heir of Bismarck when he had only inherited his immoral methods. Above all, he lacked Bismarck's confidence.

In consequence, although he would have liked to accept the British offers he shrank back from fear that Germany would become Britain's catspaw, and be converted into her shock-absorber against Russia. On the other hand he felt that Britain's weakness might now be exploited for Germany's benefit by holding Britain at arm's length and wringing concessions from her, while still keeping her hopeful of closer ties. In this view at least he was supported by the Chancellor, Bülow, and the Kaiser, whose outlook was well summed up in his words to Bülow – 'I have now got the British, despite their twisting and wriggling, where I want them.' And the German navy, expanded afresh in 1900, was the means of putting the screw on harder.

During the next few years, and especially during the South African crisis and war, the British Government had to pay heavily, not for German support, but merely for the privilege that German threats and insults should not be pressed to action. Over the Portuguese colonies, over Samoa, over China, Lord Salisbury's Government showed such contemptible weakness as almost to justify the Kaiser's description of them as 'unmitigated noodles'; the revelations from the diplomatic archives of these years are sorry reading. To them, indeed, can be traced an indirect responsibility for the eventual conflict, for it was natural that the Kaiser and his advisers should be confirmed in their good opinion of the mailed-fist method. He can be acquitted of a desire to press his method as far as actual war, not only because of the evidence of his distaste for it, but because of his tendency to superficial judgement. The limited menace was so obviously yielding the profits of war without the hazards, that the too obvious deduction was just the one to appeal to his mentality.

His responsibility for the war lies in these years. And it is a large responsibility, indeed, the largest. By the distrust and alarm which his bellicose utterances and attitude created everywhere he filled Europe with gunpowder. It is as irrational to fix the chief blame on those who eventually struck the sparks as it is to concentrate investigation of the war's origins on the brief month when the sparks were struck.

In reaction from the unhistorical propaganda which pictured the Kaiser as seeking, or even planning the war, the pendulum has swung too far the other way. To recognize his erratic good intentions should not lead us to underestimate his bad effects. And they came essentially from the fact that he was too well pleased with the reflection of his acts and himself. He saw himself arrayed in 'shining armour' when actually he was wearing the garb of Puck. He proved that making mischief makes war.

In delaying any acceptance of British overtures the Kaiser and Bülow felt secure. They underrated the effect of a common uneasiness in making easy bedfellows. With undue assurance they argued that there could be no real union 'between the whale and the bear', and by their acts they compelled this union. In retrospect, the most extraordinary feature is the number of kicks required to drive Britain away from Germany and into the awkward embrace of the Dual Alliance. Germany had at least full warning, for Chamberlain warned her in 1898 and again in 1901 that 'the period of England's splendid isolation is past ... we should prefer adherence to Germany and the Triple Alliance. But if this proves impossible then we, too, contemplate a *rapprochement* with France and Russia.'

The German belief in its impossibility proved a fallacy. That belief was summed up in Holstein's words – 'the threatened understanding with Russia and France is purely an English swindle ... A reasonable agreement with England can, in my opinion, only be attained when the feeling of compulsion over there has become more general.' He was too clever. By his 'reasonable agreement' he meant not an alliance between equals but the relation of master and servant. Weakly as the British government had behaved, and weaker still as it appeared to one imbued with the 'blood and iron' philosophy, this weakness is not sufficient to explain Holstein's amazing presumption. This is, indeed, an illustration that the real trouble in Germany, and the cause of her troubles, was not any true Machiavellian design, but merely the complaint summed up in the schoolboy phrase 'swelled head'.

Britain's first attempt to strengthen her position in other directions was her alliance with Japan in 1902. Its European significance is that it did not carry Britain away from Germany, but tended to raise a fresh barrier between Britain and the Dual Alliance. It sprang from Chamberlain's original proposal of a treaty between Britain, Germany, and

Japan, in close touch with the United States. Germany held back and so almost did Japan. For the Japanese statesman, Marquis Ito, preferred to seek an alliance with Russia, and was only turned from his purpose because his arrival in St Petersburg was outstripped by the progress of the negotiations in London between Baron Hayashi, the Japanese ambassador, and Lord Lansdowne, the Foreign Secretary. Even then, the Japanese Council of Elder statesmen wavered, under Ito's pressure, before accepting the British alliance – whose indirect result was thus to precipitate the Russo-Japanese war, a result neither desired by nor palatable to Britain.

For by 1904 a dramatic change had occurred in the European situation. Only five years before, France had been so bitter against Britain over Fashoda that she had almost forgotten Alsace-Lorraine. But fear of Germany, more deep-seated, made her statesmen open to approach when, in 1901, Chamberlain fulfilled his warning to Germany. The first step in the eventual negotiations between Lansdowne and Paul Cambon, the French Ambassador, was to remove causes of friction at the most sensitive point – overseas. The greatest obstacle was Egypt, still a cherished object of French ambition, and it was no mean diplomatic feat that recognition of Britain's actual occupation was exchanged for recognition of French right to occupy Morocco if she could. The agreement was signed in April, 1904. Although the popular idea of King Edward VII's responsibility for the agreement is purely legendary – still more so the popular German idea of him as spinning a Machiavellian web around Germany – his visit to Paris created the atmosphere in which agreement was possible. At first his reception was frigid, but his tact and understanding of the French combined with their truly republican love of royalty to hasten a thaw, and succeeding visits uncovered common ground. Thus if it is not true that he made the new *entente*, he undoubtedly made it *cordiale*.

But the Kaiser also helped. Deeply chagrined that the lover whose advances Germany had spurned had dared to woo another, his mischief-making was now redoubled. His efforts were directed to break up the Franco-British entente. And the coincident Russo-Japanese war provided the opportunity. His first move was a failure, for the peace-loving Tsar rejected his advice to send the Black Sea Fleet through the Dardanelles in defiance of Britain. But when the Baltic Fleet, Russia's last naval trump, sailed for the Far East it received false information – the Russians later alleged that it came from German sources – that Japanese torpedo craft were lying in wait in the North Sea. Through a panic mistake they fired on British trawlers, and made no effort to redeem their error, which brought Russia and Britain momentarily to the brink of war. For some days the British Channel Fleet shadowed the Russians, until the tension was eased by a message of regret from the Tsar, against the wishes of the war party in Russia. The Tsar, bitter at his humiliation, now, to the Kaiser's delight, proposed a combination of Russia, Germany, and France 'to abolish English and Japanese arrogance and insolence'. The Kaiser promptly dispatched a draft treaty between Russia and Germany, but urged the Tsar not to divulge it to the French, arguing that the 'Treaty once a *fact*, our combined powers will exert a strong attraction on France', and adding that 'an excellent expedient to cool British insolence and overbearing would be to make some military demonstration on the Perso-Afghan frontier...' But it was the Tsar who cooled, on reflection.

The next German move was singularly inapt, and for it the Kaiser was not responsible. Now, too late, he wanted to woo France instead of trying to separate her from Britain by threat. But he was sent off by Bülow and Holstein to Tangiers, there to 'throw down the glove to France' by a speech which challenged French claims in Morocco. Bülow followed it up by calling for a conference to review the future of Morocco. The challenge came at an awkward moment. The French army was suffering one of its periodical crises, Russia was entangled with Japan, and the French Prime Minister, Rouvier, doubted both the assurance and value of British support. Thus the foreign minister, Delcassé, was sacrificed and France accepted the demand. The mailed fist had scored afresh, but the alarm had driven Britain and France closer together.

The third move was the Kaiser's own. In July, 1905, when on board the Tsar's yacht at Bjorko, he suddenly produced the draft treaty, and in his hybrid 'Willy-Nicky' English, asked – 'Should you like to sign it? It would be a very nice souvenir of our *entrevue*.' The Kaiser relates that, when Nicholas answered 'Yes, I will', 'tears of joy filled my eyes – a thrill ran down my spine', and he felt that all his ancestors including 'Grandpapa' and the 'old Prussian God' were giving him their benediction. This phase of royal diplomacy, however serious its implication, was not without its humorous relief. There is a delightful commercial touch in one of his letters to 'Dearest Nicky' – 'Now that the programme for the renewal of your fleet has been published, I hope you won't forget to remind your authorities to remember our great firms at Stettin, Kiel, etc. They will, I am sure, furnish fine specimens of line of battleships.' Melodrama marks his aggrieved letter to Bülow who, as the treaty ran counter to his own anti-French aims in Morocco, threatened resignation – 'The morning after your resignation reaches him, the Kaiser will no longer be in this world! Think of my poor wife and children.'

But when the Tsar's ministers saw the treaty, they objected that it could not be reconciled with the French alliance, and sufficient hint of it leaked out to cause strong protests from France. Thus the 'masterpiece' was quietly dropped into the diplomatic waste-paper basket.

In justice to the Kaiser it must be mentioned that at the time he had some cause for personal grievance against Britain, even though it was largely the reaction to his long-standing habit of seeking his end by threats. His forceful impulsiveness had a counterpart in Sir John Fisher, just become First Sea Lord, who constantly talked of a preventive war and freely aired suggestions that if Germany would not limit her naval expansion her fleet should be 'Copenhagened' – on the Nelson model. Such wild suggestions naturally made more impression in Berlin than in London. King Edward VII's share as a cause of irritation was social and personal rather than political. A little more tolerance towards his nephew's *gaucherie* might have helped to make relations smoother. Lord Lansdowne records that 'the King talks and writes about his royal brother in terms which make one's flesh creep'. These personal antipathies and pinpricks, of little account on the British side, where the King was a constitutional ruler and also had a sense of humour, had a deeper reaction on the German side of the North Sea, where the ruler could influence policy decisively and had no sense of humour. And by inciting the Kaiser to further mischief-making intrigues and menaces they had an ultimate reaction in Britain, where even the new Liberal government of Campbell-Bannerman could not ignore them, and was unwillingly forced closer into the arms of France.

While the government refused to commit Britain to a formal alliance with France, it held out the hope that British public opinion might favour intervention if France was attacked. And when the French logically argued that emergency aid would be no use unless its method of application had been thought out, Campbell-Bannerman authorized discussions between the two general staffs. While these had no effect upon the eventual decision for war, they were to have a great influence on the conduct of the war. It is significant also that in 1905 the new German war plan made allowance for a British expeditionary force of 100,000 men – the very figure the French asked for – being present on the French side.

Balked of his idea of drawing France, with Russia, into a combination against Britain, the Kaiser now reverted to the idea of action against France over Morocco. He decided, however, that 'from a technico-military standpoint' conditions were not suitable, and that an alliance with Turkey, 'which would place the forces of Mahommedanism to the furthest extent – under Prussian leadership – at my disposal', and a secure internal position were necessary preliminaries. This illuminating example of his unbalanced mind is contained in a letter of December 31st, 1905, to Bülow, which concludes – 'First shoot the Socialists down, behead them, render them impotent – if necessary per Blood bath – and then war abroad! But not before, and not *a tempo*.'

Yet the next change in the European situation was not to strengthen his foundations, but to weaken them, by weakening his influence over Russia in the person of the Tsar. With supreme irony the change came in the most unlikely way – by the drawing together of the new British government and its antipathy, despotic Russia. Impelled partly by its general pacifism and partly by its natural reaction to German menaces, the Liberal government continued the effort begun by Lansdowne to remove the traditional sources of friction with Russia. And in 1907 the points of difference at the points of contact were settled by an arrangement. While there was no definite agreement, the natural effect was to smoothe the way to cooperation in Europe. Although Britain was not tied either to France or Russia by any formal agreement she was tied to their side by the bonds of loyalty, and so could no longer impose a check upon them without suspicion of disloyalty. Thus her old independent influence in a crisis had slipped away.

The dilemma was realized and well summed up by the Foreign Secretary, Sir Edward Grey, in a memorandum of February 20th, 1906:

'There would, I think, be a general feeling in every country that we had behaved meanly and left France in the lurch. The United States would despise us, Russia would not think it worthwhile to make a friendly arrangement with us about Asia, Japan would prepare to reinsure herself elsewhere, we should be left without a friend and without the power of making a friend and Germany would take some pleasure in exploiting the whole situation to our disadvantage ... On the other hand the prospect of a European war and of our being involved in it is horrible.'

Henceforth the great powers were in fact, if not in name, divided into two rival groups. During the next few years Germany, whose aggressive and impolitic policy had created the counter group, so curiously assorted, was also to help and be helped by Austria in hardening it, as a snowball is hardened when squeezed. But she was also to suffer from her own creation. Britain's adhesion to the new group weakened the old, by making Italy a doubtful partner. Hence Germany was compelled to cling more closely to her other partner, Austria, whom formerly she had led. If Germany wished for war, this bondage was an advantage, but if she wished for peace she would be hampered even as Britain was hampered.

The new grouping of Europe was not the old balance of power but merely a barrier between powers. That barrier, moreover, was charged with explosives – the armaments which the several countries, now driven more by fear than by ambition, hurriedly augmented. Another ill consequence was that fear of a sudden detonation led the autocratic powers at least to give the military custodians of these armaments a dangerously free hand in disposing them. Fear had taken charge of reason long before July 1914.

The first spark came from the Balkans in 1908. The revolution in Turkey was seized upon by Bulgaria to throw off Turkish suzerainty and by Austria to annex the provinces of Bosnia and Herzegovina, which she had administered since 1879. This annexation had been discussed between the Austrian and Russian foreign ministers, Ahrenthal and Isvolsky, and Isvolsky had been willing to assent to it in return for Austrian support in securing the opening of the Dardanelles. But before Isvolsky could sound France and Britain, the annexation was declared. In Italy it was justly felt to be an affront, and in Serbia to be a menace. But in Russia the effect was made worse by the German ambassador's peremptory demand that Russia should recognize it under pain of a combined Austrian and German attack.

Russia, caught when she had been acting single-handed, and threatened by a two-handed combination, gave way from fear, and was left with resentment, aggravated by the sense of having forfeited her standing in the Balkans. Isvolsky felt that he had been not only browbeaten but duped, and resigning soon after, went to the Paris embassy as an embittered foe of the Germanic powers. Another personal factor. And Austria, flattered by this first success in imitating Germany's mailed-fist method of diplomacy, was encouraged to continue it.

This Bosnian deceit of Ahrenthal's stands out predominantly among the immediate origins of the war. Its intervention was the more unfortunate because the years 1906–14 saw an improvement in Germany's official relations, at least, with France and Britain. It would have been more marked but for the continued ominous increase in the German navy. It is easy to appreciate now that the Kaiser's encouragement to Tirpitz's anti-British naval ambitions was due largely to vanity, but then it looked more naturally a consistently designed challenge. And even when he tried to repair the damage the Kaiser was unhappy in his method. His way of conciliating British feeling was to declare, in the famous *Daily Telegraph* interview of 1908, that the British were 'mad as March hares' not to recognize his friendship, and that he was in a minority in a land 'not friendly to England'. Without soothing British fears, it caused an outcry in Germany, a public repudiation by Bülow. And it thus weakened the Kaiser's own power to check the war party in Germany.

But it at least led to the Kaiser's replacement of Bülow as Chancellor by the well-meaning Bethmann-Hollweg, who was more desirous of peace if less capable of preserving it. He promptly opened negotiations for an Anglo-German agreement, and met with an eager response from the Liberal government, now renewed in power by the elections of 1910. But practical results were barred, first, by Tirpitz's opposition to any naval adjustment and, second, by the German demand that any agreement must be so worded as to bar Britain from coming to the aid of France.

This was too obviously a strategic move. Sir Edward Grey made the only possible reply – 'One does not make new friendships worth having by deserting old ones.'

Nevertheless the tension was eased. The German public, press and Kaiser – as shown by his documentary comments – still suffered from Anglophobia, owing largely to the feeling of thwarted aims and the much-propagated idea that King Edward VII had planned a vast hostile encirclement of Germany. Perhaps the most illuminating reaction was the belief that the King's 1908 visit to the Emperor Francis Joseph was a move to detach Austria from Germany, whereas we now know from the Austrian archives that the King actually asked Francis Joseph's assistance towards reducing the friction between Britain and Germany, and valued the alliance as a common link. But the discussions helped the relations between the British and German foreign ministries and led them to cooperate in settling several points of dispute. Relations were also helped by the settlement between France and Germany over Morocco.

Characteristically, this settlement followed a new crisis. The crisis, curiously enough, was provoked by the otherwise pacific Foreign Minister, Kiderlen-Wächter, and opposed by the Kaiser, another instance of that incalculable double-headedness which was so dangerous a feature of German policy. As a means of encouraging France to grant concessions in Africa, in June, 1911, Kiderlen-Wächter dispatched a gunboat to Agadir. In reply, Lloyd George, the former opponent of the Boer War and the leading pacifist in the British Cabinet, warned Germany in a public speech against such threats to peace. The effect, in conjunction with firm indications of a readiness to support France, was to damp the spark. But resentment made public opinion in Germany more combustible than ever, and it enthusiastically approved yet another increase in the German Navy. Nevertheless, the subsequent settlement over Morocco removed a serious source of friction between France and Germany, and thus indirectly contributed to the better official atmosphere in which Haldane's 1912 mission to Germany took place. Yet even Haldane had to confess that his 'spiritual home' had become a 'powder magazine', although he communicated his fears only to his colleagues in the Cabinet. The growth of the war party in Germany, however, was accompanied by a consolidation of the peace elements, most marked among the Socialists, and the presence of a pacifically minded Chancellor kept open a possible avenue for further negotiations.

But at this very time a fresh powder trail was laid – in the Balkans. The weakness of Turkey, and the example of Italy in occupying Tripoli, encouraged Bulgaria, Serbia, and Greece to claim autonomy for Macedonia as a step to ejecting the Turks from Europe. The Turks were quickly defeated. Serbia's share of the spoils was to be Northern Albania. But Austria, already fearful of Serb ambitions, had no intention of allowing a Slav state to gain access to the Adriatic. She mobilized her troops and her threat to Serbia was naturally answered by Russia's similar preparations. Fortunately, Germany joined with Britain and France to forestall the danger. Less fortunately, their settlement was the cause of a fresh crisis. For, by setting up Albania as an independent state, they upset the division of the spoil. Serbia now claimed part of Macedonia; Bulgaria refused not only by word but by blow, only to be overcome by the combined weight of Serbia and Greece, while Rumania joined in, and Turkey slipped back to recover her lost property under cover of the dust raised by the 'dog-fight'.

As a result Serbia was the chief gainer and Bulgaria the chief loser. This was much to Austria's distaste and in the summer of the 1913 she proposed an immediate attack on Serbia. Germany restrained her, counselling moderation, but herself gave Russia a fresh cause of offence by extending German control of the Turkish Army. Russia saw her dream of the Dardanelles fading, and her ministers came to the conclusion that it could only be revived if a general European war occurred – a dangerful attitude of mind. Their immediate aim was now to recover their shaken influence in the Balkans, and they sought to win over Rumania as a first step towards building a new Balkan alliance. The prospect created fresh alarm in Austria, already distracted by the internal strain of her diverse racial parts.

Force was her method to suppress the dissatisfaction of her Serb and Croat subjects in the annexed provinces and of her Rumanian subjects in Transylvania. And her desire was to apply the same remedy in time to the external state – Serbia – which formed a natural rallying point for all the dissatisfied elements within. Her leaders felt that war beyond her frontiers would be the best way to silence discord within. In this feeling they were not alone. The popular unrest in Russia, only half stifled by the use of knout and exile, and the clamour for universal suffrage in Germany, made the war parties in both countries look to war as a safety-valve.

During the last year incitements multiplied on all sides – bellicose speeches, articles, rumours, frontier incidents. President Wilson's confidant, Colonel House, left Berlin with the conviction that the military party was determined on war, at the earliest opportunity, and would force the Kaiser to abdicate if he opposed their desire. Their excitement was certainly aggravated by the Three Years' Service Act which France had passed as a remedy for her inferior man power in face of recent developments in the German Army. But the German ambassador reported to Bethmann-Hollweg that: 'In spite of the chauvinistic attitude of many circles and the general dream of a recovery of the lost provinces, the French nation as a whole could be described as desirous of peace.' The most that could be said, even of Poincaré, the President, was what Poincaré himself expressed, 'that France did not want war, but did not fear it'. Elsewhere, however, the surface of the continent was now strewn with powder. And everywhere the air was heavy with fatalism.

The fatal spark was struck at Serajevo, the Bosnian capital, on June 28th, 1914. Its first victim marked the irony of destiny. The fiery Slav nationalists who sought to advance their cause by murdering the Archduke Franz Ferdinand, the heir to Francis Joseph, singled out the one man of influence in Austria who was their friend. For Franz Ferdinand also had dreams – of a reconstructed empire in which the several nationalities were held together not in bondage but in federation. But to most of the Bosnian Slavs he was merely the symbol of the oppressor, and to the extreme nationalists who plotted his death he was the more to be hated because his dream of reconciliation within the empire might thwart theirs of breaking away from the empire, to join with Serbia in creating a wider Yugo-Slav state.

The handful of youthful conspirators sought and received help from the Serbian secret society known as the 'Black Hand'. This was largely composed of army officers, who formed a group hostile to the existing civil government in Serbia. Rumours of the conspiracy seem to have reached the ears of ministers, and orders were sent to the frontier to intercept the conspirators, but as the frontier guards were members of the 'Black Hand' the precautions naturally failed. It seems also, but is not certain, that a vague warning was sent to Vienna. What is certain is the amazing carelessness of the Austrian authorities in guarding the Archduke, and their cynical indifference to the fate that befell this highly unpopular heir to the throne. Potiorek, the military governor of Bosnia and future commander of the offensive against Serbia, could not have done more to facilitate the task of the assassins if he had connived at it. Hence there must always be a suspicion that he did.

After a first attempt, on the Archduke's passage to the city hall, had failed, Potiorek so clumsily directed the return journey that the Archduke's car had to pull up, and two shots rang out, mortally wounding the Archduke and his court-despised morganatic consort. He died at 11 AM – a prophetic hour.

The news of the crime caused horror and indignation in all countries save two – Austria and Serbia. The Serbian press made little effort to conceal its pleasure, and the Serbian public still less, while the government which, exhausted by the Balkan wars, had every incentive for peace in order to consolidate its gains, was foolishly remiss in making or offering an investigation into the complicity of its subjects.

Austrian police investigation was also leisurely, and after a fortnight Wiesner, who was deputed to conduct it, reported that while Serbian societies and officials were implicated there were 'no proofs of the complicity of the Serbian government ... On the contrary there are grounds for believing it quite out of the question.'

But Austrian decision was prompt, although any outward appearance of action was long delayed. Count Berchtold, the Foreign Minister – who had added an air of elegance to the tradition of deceit bequeathed by Ahrenthal – gracefully and gratefully seized the opportunity to retrieve Austria's and his own lost prestige. The day after the crime he declared to the Chief of the General Staff that the time had come to settle with Serbia once for all – words that seemed to Conrad von Hötzendorf the echo of his own repeated promptings to war. But Berchtold met an unexpected obstacle in Count Tisza, who objected strongly, on the score of expediency, not of morality – 'There can be no difficulty in finding a suitable *casus belli* whenever it is needed.' Conrad also considered expediency and remarked to Berchtold – 'We must above all ask Germany whether she is willing to safeguard us against Russia.' Berchtold, too, had no wish to meet a rebuff from Germany such as so damaged his prestige two years before. Hence the aged Emperor was induced to sign a memorandum for the Kaiser, accompanied by a personal letter.

But the Kaiser needed no appeal. For when the German ambassador, Tschirschky, had sent off a report of his conversation with Berchtold on June 30th, saying that he had given a warning against hasty steps, the Kaiser scribbled in the margin – 'Who authorized him to do this? It is idiotic. It is none of his business ... Tschirschky must be good enough to stop this lunacy. We must clear the Serbians out of the way, and that too forthwith.' Poor Tschirschky, he was not equal to his master's somersaults. Formerly energetic in incitement, he presumably remembered his master's voice, urging restraint two years before, and now thought that he was fulfilling the Kaiser's wish by changing his own tune – only to find that the Kaiser had also changed. How shall we explain it? Most probably by the Kaiser's fear of being again reproached with weakness and by his characteristic indignation that royal blood had been shed, if also by the more creditable motive of his friendship with the murdered man.

Thus to Count Hoyos, the Austrian letter-bearer, he gave the assurance, on July 5th, that Austria 'could depend on the complete support of Germany'. 'In the Kaiser's opinion there must be no delay ... if it was to come to a war between Austria-Hungary and Russia she could be assured that Germany would stand at her side', although he added that Russia 'was in no way ready for war'. Germany was – so he was assured. In a series of hasty consultations with his military and naval advisers, various precautionary measures were ordered. Meantime, the Kaiser left, as arranged, to visit Norway. A few days later, on the 17th, Waldersee, the Assistant Chief of the General Staff, reported to the Foreign Minister – 'I shall remain here ready to jump. We are all prepared.'

This blank cheque, endorsed by the Chancellor and given with full recognition of the consequences, stands out predominant among the immediate causes of the war. Austria hurried to cash it, and Tschirschky was only too eager to repair his blunder in urging caution. Unlike later decisions this was taken in a calm if not a cool atmosphere, a fact which gives it special significance in assessing the will to war. Significant also is the care taken by Germany and Austria to lull suspicion of any impending move – in Conrad's words, 'peaceful intentions should be simulated'. While giving no advice to Austria to keep her demands within moderation, the German government showed its anxiety that the support of Italy, Bulgaria, Rumania and Turkey should be ensured for a war. Italy was to be given no hint of the action intended, but Austria was urged to be ready with a price for her support when war came.

Now assured of Germany's backing, Berchtold's next problem is so to draft the ultimatum to Serbia that it will be unacceptable. This takes some thought and on July 10th Berchtold confesses to Tschirschky that he is still considering 'what demands could be put that it would be wholly impossible for Serbia to accept'. The only dissenting voice is that of Tisza, but he is told – 'A diplomatic success would be valueless.' He threatens to withhold his support, but suddenly veers round – after Berchtold has warned him of 'the military difficulties which would be caused by a delay', and has impressed the fact that 'Germany would not understand any neglect on our part to use this opportunity for striking a blow'. Austria might forfeit her partnership with Germany if she showed weakness.

The ultimatum is drawn up, and after reading it the old Emperor says – 'Russia cannot accept this ... this means a general war.' But its delivery is delayed until various war preparations are complete – and Poincaré has sailed from St Petersburg, where he has been visiting the Tsar. The Russian ambassador in Vienna is also induced by peaceful assurances to go on leave. But the German steamship lines are warned of the date on which the Austrian note would be delivered, and that they must be ready for swift 'developments'.

At 6 PM on July 23rd the ultimatum is presented to the Serbian government – when the Prime Minister is away. Its terms not only demand the repression of all propaganda against Austria, but Austria's right to order the dismissal of any Serbian officials that she cares to name and to post her own officials in Serbia. This directly violates Serbia's status as an independent country. Only forty-eight hours are allowed for acceptance. Next day the German government delivers notes in St Petersburg, Paris and London, which state that the Austrian demands are 'moderate and proper' – the German government had not even seen the ultimatum when it light-heartedly wrote this – and add the threat that 'any interference ... would be followed by incalculable consequences'. In London the note caused stupefaction, in Russia fierce indignation.

But, two minutes before the ultimatum expired the Serbian reply was handed to the Austrian ambassador. Without waiting to read it, he broke off relations and caught the train from Belgrade, in accordance with his instructions. Formal orders were issued three hours later for Austria's partial mobilization – on the Serbian front. Simultaneously preparatory measures for mobilization took place in Germany and Russia.

Yet the Serbian note had accepted all the Austrian demands except the two which definitely violated her independence. When the Kaiser read it, on July 28th, after his return, he wrote the comment – 'A brilliant performance for a time limit of only forty-eight hours ... A great moral victory for Vienna; but with it every reason for war drops away.' And in reference to Austria's partial mobilization he adds – 'On the strength of this I should never have ordered mobilization.' Once more the mailed fist has triumphed and the Kaiser, having shown the doubters that he is a strong man, is eager to rest on his laurels. Royal honour is satisfied. But he unwisely suggests that Austria might well occupy part of Serbia until her demands are fulfilled – an act that Russia could never be expected to permit. Bethmann-Hollweg agreed with the Kaiser's view, and on the morning of the 28th the advice was sent to Vienna, adding that, 'If Austria continues her refusal to all proposals for mediation or arbitration, the odium of being responsible for a world war will in the eyes of the German people fall on the German Government.'

But the changed tone was fatally belated. Germany had herself blocked these proposals during the most auspicious period. When the German note was delivered, on July 24th, Russia was at once assured of France's support, and Grey was pressed by his allies to declare Britain's solidarity with them. But his parliamentary responsibility and the divided views of the Cabinet, as well as the uncertainty of public support, hindered any such declaration. He feared, too, that any such action might strengthen the war parties in Russia and Germany. Instead, he tried to open a path to mediation. His first move, on the 24th, was to urge through Berlin an extension of the Austrian time limit. It received no support in Berlin and was tardily passed on to Vienna where it arrived two hours before the expiration, when it was at once rejected. On the 25th and 26th he made further proposals for joint mediation by Germany, Britain, France and Italy, while Austria, Russia, and Serbia were to abstain from military operations. Prompt acceptance came at once from Paris and Rome. Sazonov in St Petersburg, who had originally mooted the idea, now agreed in principle but preferred first to try direct discussions with Vienna. Berlin refused. The Kaiser scribbled his usual incendiary comments on the reports that came to him – 'That is a tremendous piece of British insolence. I am not called upon to prescribe *à la* Grey to HM the Emperor [of Austria] how to preserve his honour.' There is much evidence that German opinion was encouraged by Britain's attitude to count on her neutrality in case of war. But in the newspapers of July 27th the British government published the news that the fleet, assembled for manoeuvres, had been ordered not to disperse. This hint in combination with the nature of Serbia's reply caused a change of official tone in Berlin – where, the day before, the General Staff had sent to the Foreign Office the ultimatum they had drafted in readiness for delivery to Belgium.

Thus, later on July 27th, the German government decided to pass Grey's proposals on to Vienna. They sent Grey word that this action implied that they 'associate themselves to a certain extent with your hope'. But after seeing the German Foreign Minister, the Austrian Ambassador telegraphed to Vienna – 'The German government offers the most unqualified assurances that it in no way identifies itself with them, but on the contrary is decidedly opposed to their consideration, and only communicates them in order to satisfy the English ... The German government is so acting because its point of view is that it is of the utmost importance that England, at the present moment, should not make common cause with Russia and France.' On the 28th, after the Kaiser had seen Serbia's reply, there was a further cooling of tone as we have seen. But Bethmann-Hollweg's cautionary message, his first, to Vienna that day was too late and too tepid.

For at 11 AM – again! – on July 28th, Austria's telegraphed declaration of war was delivered to Serbia. And the same day Berchtold refused Sazonov's proposal for direct conversations, giving as his reason the fact that war was now declared! A grim humour underlies both the cause and method of Austria's precipitate decision. Militarily there was every reason for delay in the actual declaration, as the army could not be ready to move until August 12th. But messages from Germany had been inciting Austria to haste; Berchtold and Conrad feared to lose her support and the chance of war if they dallied. Berchtold cynically summed up the position to the Emperor on July 27th – 'I think that a further attempt by the Entente Powers to bring about a peaceful solution remains possible only so long as a new situation has not been created by the declaration of war.' And in obtaining the Emperor's signature to the declaration of war, he quenched any doubts by incorporating the justification that Serbian had attacked Austrian troops.

Having achieved his end, he then deleted the sentence referring to this imaginary attack!

The rush to the abyss now gathered unbrakable speed – driven by the motor of 'military necessity'. In constructing their huge and cumbrous machines the general staffs of Europe had forgotten the first principle of war – elasticity. Alike in mobilization and in use the conscript armies of the Continent were almost unmanageable. Events were soon to show that they could be set in motion, but could not be effectively guided; their steering lock was inadequate. In this deficiency, now a danger to peace, they afforded a contrast both to the fleets of the time and to the small professional armies of the past.

The one thought of the Generals during these critical days was to start their machines. Desire for war, and fear, of being caught at a disadvantage, reacted on each other. Thus in Germany and Russia, as already in Austria, any desire among the statesmen for peace suffered the counter pull of the Generals' entreaties to action, and predictions of dire consequences if their technical advice was disregarded. Already in Austria, the Generals shared with Berchtold the sombre distinction of having initiated the war.

Their next success was in Russia – also a land of military mediocrity. There, the news of the Austrian declaration of war wrought a decisive change. Hitherto Sazonov had kept the Generals in hand. Now he begins to succumb to inevitability, and suggests that partial mobilization shall be carried out – of the troops on the Austrian front only. The General Staff argue that for 'technical reasons' this is impracticable, and urge that only a general mobilization can avoid upsetting the machine. Unwilling to yield to their arguments, yet unwilling to override them, Sazonov makes a compromise. Two *ukases* are prepared for the Tsar's signature, one for partial and one for general mobilization, and a decision between them is put off.

But the General Staff are working on the second. Next morning, the chief of the mobilization branch receives the order for general mobilization signed provisionally by the Tsar, and goes round to obtain the necessary signature of the ministers. One of them cannot be found until the evening. Meantime the German ambassador calls on Sazonov, about 6 PM, and gives him a message from Bethmann-Hollweg, that – 'If Russia continues her mobilization measures Germany will mobilize, and mobilization means war.' The message is delivered with the assurance that it is 'not a threat, but a friendly opinion'; to Sazonov it sounds more like a threat, and it seems to prohibit even partial mobilization on the Austrian frontier. His opposition to his own clamorous

General Staff weakens, and after a conference with its chief, Yanushkevich, he apparently consents to general mobilization and obtains the
Tsar's approval.

Let us shift our gaze for a moment to Berlin. There the same nervous
tension exists and the same tug of wills is in progress. But the Kaiser
and his political advisers are now seriously alarmed that Austria's
action will make them appear the guilty party, and so cost them the
support of Italy while ensuring the entry of Britain against them. Thus
a demand of the General Staff for immediate mobilization is refused,
and late in the evening Bethmann-Hollweg sees the British ambassador.
He tries to bargain for Britain's neutrality and suggests that in return
Germany would not annex any part of France – but he 'cannot give him
such an assurance' as regards the French colonies. The ambassador tells
him that acceptance of the offer is highly improbable, wherein he
proves a true prophet. Lichnowsky's warnings from London, that
British opinion is hardening, send the Kaiser into a paroxysm of
frightened rage. He scrawls abusive epithets about 'English pharisaism',
calling Grey 'a mean deceiver', and, rather oddly in view of Bethmann-
Hollweg's offer, terms the British a 'pack of base hucksters'. But
Lichnowsky's report of Grey's renewed proposals for mediation at least
induces Bethmann-Hollweg to send a string of telegrams to Vienna ex-
horting the Austrians not to continue their open refusal, lest they drag
Germany into war at a disadvantage. The Kaiser, also, telegraphs to the
Tsar saying that he is trying to persuade Vienna to agree to 'frank
negotiations'. It crosses a similar conciliatory telegram from the Tsar,
and is answered by a second, suggesting that – 'It would be right to give
over the Austro-Serbian problem to the Hague Conference. I trust in
your wisdom and friendship.' The fact that the Kaiser's marginal comment is 'Rubbish' casts a doubt upon his sincerity. But the Kaiser has
also sent a second telegram of appeal to check military measures which
'would precipitate a calamity . . .' This produces an actual effect.

The Tsar, about 10 PM, rings up the Chief of Staff, and despite
Yanushkevich's horrified protests that the orders have now gone out,
directs him to cancel them and substitute a partial mobilization.

But the General Staff, though discomfited, are not defeated. Next
morning, in order to retrieve the position, they bring fresh arguments
and all their weight to bear. First they try to approach the Tsar, but he
takes refuge from their pressure by refusing to see the Minister of War.
Yanushkevich then seeks out Sazonov, and insists that any further delay
in general mobilization will 'dislocate' the army organization and en-
danger Russia's safety. He further contends that partial mobilization

will give the French the impression that, when war came, Russia will be unable to help her in resisting Germany's onslaught. Sazonov, now resigned to the certainty of war, agrees to visit the Tsar that afternoon. The Tsar, pale and worried, gives way and gives the order – after Sazonov has soothingly assured him that whatever happens his conscience will be clear. Sazonov telephones the order to Yanushkevich, and advises him to 'disappear for the rest of the day', as a safeguard against the Tsar's vacillation. Sazonov first thinks of trying to keep the general mobilization as secret as possible, without issuing any proclamation, but finds it technically impossible, and the *ukase* is posted up next morning, July 31st. That same day, but a few hours later, the Austrian order for general mobilization is given. Henceforth the 'statesmen' may continue to send telegrams, but they are merely waste paper. The military machine has completely taken charge.

Indeed, it had done so on the 30th – not only in Russia. At 2 PM Moltke, the Chief of the German General Staff, had sent a message to the Austrian General Staff through their attaché that Russia's military measure 'will develop into a *casus foederis* for Germany ... Decline the renewed advances of Great Britain in the interest of peace. A European war is the last chance of saving Austria-Hungary. Germany is ready to back Austria unreservedly.' Subsequently he sent a telegram direct to Conrad – 'Mobilize at once against Russia. Germany will mobilize. Persuade Italy, by offering compensation, to do her duty as an ally.' Thus Moltke counteracted the irresolute telegrams of Bethmann-Hollweg. The Austrian military and civil leaders needed no urging, merely the assurance of Germany's support, and had no intention of acceding to any proposals for mediation unless Germany threatened to withdraw that support. And 'Germany' now meant the General Staff.

As soon as news reached Berlin of the Russian order, a 'state of danger of war' was proclaimed, which comprised the first step of mobilization – a neat military device to gain a lead without giving away a trick. At the same time ultimatums were dispatched both to St Petersburg and Paris. The ultimatum to Russia demanded that she 'must suspend every war measure against Austria and ourselves within twelve hours', and 'definitely notify us of this'. Sazonov, in reply, said that it was technically impossible to stop the mobilization but that, so long as negotiations continued, Russia would not attack. The Tsar reinforced this statement with another telegram to the Kaiser – 'Understand that you are obliged to mobilize, but wish to have the same guarantee from you as I gave you that these measures do not mean war, and that we shall continue negotiating ...' But, without waiting to hear the reply to their ultimatum, the German government dispatched a formally worded declaration of war to their ambassador in St Petersburg, who duly delivered it, after the expiry of the time limit, in the early evening of August 1st. Almost coincidently German mobilization began.

Yet General von Chelius had shrewdly reported from St Petersburg – 'People have mobilized here through fear of coming events with no aggressive purpose, and are already terrified at the result.' And the Kaiser had made the note – 'Right; that is the truth.' But the Kaiser, now equally frightened, and willing, could not stop his own military machine. For Moltke was insistent that 'the unusually favourable situation should be used to strike', pointing out that 'France's military situation is nothing less than embarrassed, that Russia is anything but confident; moreover, the time of year is favourable'. The rashness of the Russian General Staff might at least be excused by 'nerves', but hardly Moltke's. If three men can be singled out as the main personal causes of the war, at this time, they are Berchtold, Conrad and Moltke. But Moltke was really a limited company – the Great General Staff.

Yet, if their action was deliberate, fear was the background of their thought, not merely militaristic ambition. Fear, among the Austrian General Staff, of the doubling of the Serbian Army in consequence of Serbia's gain of territory in the Balkan war. Fear, among the German General Staff, of the Russian Army's unexpectedly rapid recovery, from its 1905 sickness under the ministrations of Sukhomlinov. Like a hard-pressed hero of the towpath, Moltke now pushed Austria into war so that he could jump in to her rescue, and then be sure of her help in return.

The German ultimatum to France demanded to know whether France would remain neutral 'in a Russo-German war', gave her eighteen hours for a reply, and added the menace, 'Mobilization will inevitably mean war'. In case she offered to remain neutral, the German ambassador was instructed to make the impossible demand that France must hand over the fortresses of Verdun and Toul as a pledge. For Moltke's plans were made for a two-front war, and his aim would be upset if only one target appeared! Could military folly go further?

The German ambassador called for his answer on August 1st, and was simply told that France 'would act as her interests required'. That afternoon the French mobilization was ordered, but in republican France the civil government was still superior to the General Staff, and since July 30th the frontier forces had been withdrawn to a line ten kilometres inside the frontier as a pacific gesture and a safeguard against the danger that a frontier skirmish might provide an excuse for war. If a military handicap, the political wisdom of this withdrawal was seen in the fact that German patrols crossed the actual frontier on the 30th and again, by German official admission, on the 31st. Thus when, on August 3rd Germany declared war on France, she could only allege the one concrete excuse that a French aviator had 'thrown bombs on the railway near Karlsruhe and Nuremberg' – a rumour already contradicted in Germany before the declaration was delivered.

Why was the actual declaration delayed two days in delivery? First, because of the fresh suggestion from Grey that so long as there was any chance of agreement between Russia and Austria, Germany and France should refrain from any attack. The suggestion was vaguely worded and Lichnowsky, in his eager desire for peace, enlarged it in telegraphing to Berlin that 'this would appear to mean that in case we did not attack France, England would remain neutral and would guarantee France's neutrality'. The Kaiser and his Chancellor clutched at the straw. The former said to Moltke – 'We march, then, with all our forces, only towards the east.' Moltke, as his memoirs relate, replied, 'that this was impossible. The advance of armies formed of millions of men ... was the result of years of painstaking work. Once planned, it could not possibly be changed.' The Kaiser bitterly retorted – 'Your uncle would have given me a different reply.' Moltke gained his way as regards the continued concentration against France, but a twenty-four hour brake was ordered to be put on the actual crossing of the frontier of France and Luxembourg. Moltke pathetically records – 'It was a great shock to me, as though something had struck at my heart.' However his heart attack was soon relieved, for late that evening further telegrams from London showed that Britain was not promising neutrality. The brake was released. And if it had caused some check on Moltke's arrangements, some of his advanced troops had actually entered Luxembourg that day in advance of timetable!

Nevertheless the British Cabinet was still wavering. A majority of its members were so anxious for peace and uncertain of the public attitude that they had failed to give a clear warning which might have strengthened Bethmann-Hollweg in his feeble efforts to withstand his own war party. Now it was too late and the military machine was in control. Nothing could have averted war after July 31st. Thus the British Cabinet's continued uncertainty, however natural and creditable, merely increased the anxiety of France, fearful of desertion.

Germany came to the rescue. Her long-prepared ultimatum to Belgium, demanding a free passage for her troops as required by her still longer-prepared war plan, was delivered on the evening of August 2nd. The Belgian government sturdily refused to allow its neutrality to be violated. On the morning of August 4th, the German troops began their invasion. The threat, even before the act was known, was decisive in hardening British opinion to the point of intervention, even though that intervention was already inevitable, as the German Staff had correctly calculated. An ultimatum was delivered that Germany should respect Belgian neutrality, and was received by Bethmann-Hollweg with the pitiful complaint that Britain was going to war 'just for a scrap of paper'. At 11 PM – by German time – the ultimatum expired. Britain also was in the war – and Italy was out of it, having already decided for neutrality on July 31st.

Thus in the final act, as in the earlier acts, 'technical military arguments' were decisive. The German army *must* go through Belgium, even though with the certainty that Britain would thereby be drawn in against Germany. Military technique – how competent in peace to gain war; how impotent in war to gain victory, so it was soon to prove!

CHAPTER TWO

The Opposing Forces

The nations entered upon the conflict with the conventional outlook and system of the eighteenth century merely modified by the events of the nineteenth century. Politically, they conceived it to be a struggle between rival coalitions based on the traditional system of diplomatic alliances, and militarily a contest between professional armies – swollen, it is true, by the continental system of conscription, yet essentially fought out by soldiers while the mass of the people watched, from seats in the amphitheatre, the efforts of their champions. The Germans had a glimpse of the truth, but – one or two prophetic minds apart – the 'Nation in Arms' theory, evolved by them during the nineteenth century, visualized the nation as a reservoir to pour its reinforcements into the army, rather than as a mighty river in which are merged many tributary forces of which the army is but one. Their conception was the 'Nation in Arms', hardly the 'Nation at War'. Even today this fundamental truth has yet to be grasped in its entirety and its full implications understood. Progressively throughout the years 1914–18 the warring nations enlisted the research of the scientist, the inventive power and technical skill of the engineer, the manual labour of industry, and the pen of the propagandist. For long this fusion of many forces tended to a chaotic maelstrom of forces; the old order had broken down, the new had not yet evolved. Only gradually did a working cooperation emerge, and it is a moot point whether even in the last phase cooperation of forces had attained to the higher level of coordination – direction by unity of diversity.

The German army of 1914 was born in the Napoleonic Wars, nursed in infancy by Gneisenau and Scharnhorst, and guided in adolescence by the elder Moltke and Roon. It reached maturity in the war of 1870, when it emerged triumphantly from a trial against the ill-equipped and badly led long-service army of France. Every physically able citizen was liable to service; the State took the number it desired, trained them to arms for a short period of full-time service, and then returned them to civil life. The feature, as also the object, of the system, was the production of a huge reserve by which to expand the active army in war. A man served two or three years full-time, according to his branch of the service, followed by five or four years in the regular reserves. He then served in the Landwehr for twelve years, and finally passed into the Landsturm from the age of thirty-nine till forty-five. Further, an Ersatz reserve was formed of those who were not called on for service with the colours.

In this organization and in the thoroughness of the training lay the secret of the first great surprise of the war, one which almost proved decisive. For instead of regarding their reservists as troops of doubtful quality, fit only for an auxiliary role or garrison duty, the Germans during mobilization were able to duplicate almost every first-line army corps with a reserve corps – and had the courage, justified by events, to use them in the opening clash. This surprise upset the French calculations and thereby dislocated their entire plan of campaign.

The Germans have been reproached for many miscalculations; less than justice has been done to the correctness of many of their intuitions. They alone realized what is today an axiom – that, given a highly trained cadre of leaders, a military machine can be rapidly manufactured from short-time levies, like molten liquid poured into a mould. The German mould was a long-service body of officers and NCOs who in their standard of technical knowledge and skill had no equal on the Continent. But if the machine was manufactured by training it gained solidity from another process. The psychological element plays an even greater part in a 'national' than in a professional army. *Esprit de corps* is not enough; the stimulus of a great moral impulse to action is necessary, a deep-rooted belief in the policy for which citizens are called on to fight. The leaders of Germany had worked for generations to inspire their people with a patriotic conviction of the grandeur of their country's destiny. And if their opponents went forth to battle in 1914 with as intense a belief in their country's cause, this flaming patriotism had not the time to consolidate such a disciplined combination as years of steady heat had produced in Germany. The German people had an intimacy with and a pride in their army, notwithstanding the severity of its discipline, that was unknown elsewhere.

This unique instrument was handled by a general staff which, by rigour of selection and training, was unmatched for professional knowledge and skill, if subject to the mental 'grooves' which characterize all professions. Executive skill is the fruit of practice; and constant practice, or repetition, tends inevitably to deaden originality and elasticity of mind. In a professional body, also, promotion by seniority is a rule difficult to avoid. The Germans, it is true, tended towards a system of staff control, which in practice usually left the real power in the hands of youthful general staff officers. As war memoirs and documents reveal, the chiefs of staff of the various armies and corps often took momentous decisions with hardly a pretence of consulting their commanders. But such a system had grave objections, and from it came the grit in the wheels which not infrequently marred the otherwise well-oiled working of the German war machine.

Tactically the Germans began with two important material advantages. They alone had gauged the potentialities of the heavy howitzer, and had provided adequate numbers of this weapon. And if no army had fully realized that machine guns were 'concentrated essence of infantry', nor fully developed this preponderant source of fire power, the Germans had studied it more than other armies, and were able to exploit its inherent power of dominating a battlefield sooner than other armies. In this anticipation of the value of heavy artillery and machine guns the German General Staff seems to have been largely influenced by the acute diagnosis of Captain Hoffmann, its youthful attaché with the Japanese Army in Manchuria. Strategically, also, the Germans had brought the study and development of railway communications to a higher pitch than any of their rivals.

The Austro-Hungarian army, if patterned on the German model, was a vastly inferior instrument. Not only had it a tradition of defeat rather than of victory, but its racial mixture prevented the moral homogeneity that distinguished its ally. This being so, the replacement of the old professional army by one based on universal service lowered rather than raised its standard of effectiveness. The troops within the borders of the empire were often racially akin to those beyond, and this compelled Austria to a politically instead of a militarily based distribution of forces, so that kinsmen should not fight each other. And her human handicap was increased by a geographical one, namely, the vast extent of frontier to be defended.

Nor were her leaders, with rare exceptions, the professional equals of the Germans. Moreover, if common action was better understood than among the Entente Powers, Austria did not accept German direction gladly.

Yet despite all its evident weaknesses the loosely knit conglomeration of races withstood the shock and strain of war for four years, in a way that surprised and dismayed her opponents. The explanation is that the complex racial fabric was woven on a stout Germanic and Magyar framework.

From the Central we turn to the Entente Powers. France possessed but sixty per cent of the potential man power of Germany (5,940,000 against 9,750,000), and this debit balance had forced her to call on the services of practically every able-bodied male. A man was called up at twenty, did three years' full-time service, then eleven in the reserve and finally two periods of seven years each in the Territorial Army and Territorial Reserve. This system gave France an initial war strength of nearly four million trained men, compared with Germany's five; but she placed little reliance on the fighting value of reservists. The French command counted only on the semi-professional troops of the first line, about 1,000,000 men, for the short and decisive campaign which they expected and prepared for. Moreover, they assumed a similar attitude on the part of their enemy – with dire result. But this initial surprise apart, a more profound handicap was the lesser capacity of France for expansion, in case of a long war, due to her smaller population – under 40,000,000 compared with Germany's 65,000,000. Colonel Mangin, later to become famous, had advocated tapping the resources in Africa, the raising of a huge native army, but the Government had considered the dangers to outweigh the advantages of such a policy, and war experience was to show that it had military as well as political risks.

The French General Staff, if less technically perfect than the German, had produced some of the most renowned military thinkers in Europe, and its level of intelligence could well bear comparison. But the French military mind tended to lose in originality and elasticity what it gained in logic. In the years preceding the war, too, a sharp division of thought had arisen which did not make for combined action. Worse still, the new French philosophy of war, by its preoccupation with the moral element, had become more and more separated from the inseparable material factors. Abundance of will cannot compensate a definite inferiority of weapons, and the second factor, once realized, inevitably reacts on the first. In material, the French had one great asset in their quick-firing 75mm field gun, the best in the world, but its very value had led them to undue confidence in a war of movement and a consequent neglect of equipment and training for the type of warfare which came to pass.

Russia's assets were in the physical sphere, her defects in the mental and moral. If her initial strength was no greater than that of Germany, her man-power resources were immense. Moreover the courage and endurance of her troops were famous. But corruption and incompetence permeated her leadership, her rank and file lacked the intelligence and initiative for scientific warfare – they formed an instrument of great solidity but little flexibility – while her manufacturing resources for equipment and munitions were far below those of the great industrial powers. This handicap was made worse by her geographical situation, for she was cut off from her allies by ice- or enemy-bound seas, and she had to cover immense land frontiers. Another radical defect was the poverty of her rail communications, which were the more essential as she relied for success on bringing into play the weight of her numbers. In the moral sphere Russia's condition was less clear. Her internal troubles were notorious and must be a brake on her efforts unless the cause was such as to make a crusade-like appeal to her primitive and incoherent masses.

Between the military systems of Germany, Austria, France and Russia there was a close relation; the differences were of detail rather than fundamental; and this similarity threw into greater contrast the system of the other great European power – Britain. Throughout modern times she had been essentially a sea power, intervening on land through a traditional policy of diplomatic and financial support to Allies, whose military efforts she reinforced with a leaven from her own professional army. This regular army was primarily maintained for the protection and control of the overseas dependencies – India in particular – and had always been kept down to the minimum strength for this purpose. The reason for the curious contrast between Britain's determination to maintain a supreme navy and her consistent neglect, indeed starvation, of the army lay partly in her insular position, which caused her to regard the sea as her essential life-line and main defence, and partly in a constitutional distrust of the army, an illogical prejudice, which had its almost forgotten source in the military government of Cromwell. Small as to size, it enjoyed a practical and varied experience of war without parallel among the continental armies. Compared with them, its obvious professional handicap was that the leaders, however apt in handling small columns in colonial expeditions, had never been prepared to direct large formations in *la grande guerre*.

But the value of such practice, and the British handicap, are easily overrated by the layman. For experience has tended to show that the larger the force, the smaller the scope for generalship, and the less the call upon it. Compared with the manifold personal initiative of a Marlborough or a Napoleon before and during battle, the decisions of an army commander in 1914–18 were necessarily few and broad – his role was more akin to that of managing director of a vast department store.

And in a war where all the leaders were soon out of their depth, and slow to recover, practical acumen counted for more than the theoretical technique acquired in peacetime exercises. These, especially in the French Army, too often bred the delusion that the issue of an order at a distance was equivalent to its fulfilment on the spot.

In the little British Army which originally took the field, personality had for a time more scope. And much was to depend upon it. Unfortunately, the issue was to suggest that the process of selection had not succeeded in bringing to the fore the officers best fitted for leadership. It is significant that, on the way out to France, Haig spoke to Charteris (his military secretary and future chief intelligence officer) of his qualms concerning the Commander-in-Chief, Sir John French, whose right hand he had been in South Africa: 'D.H. unburdened himself today. He is greatly concerned about the composition of British GHQ. He thinks French quite unfit for high command in time of crisis ... He says French's military ideas are not sound; that he has never studied war; that he is obstinate, and will not keep with him men who point out even obvious errors. He gives him credit for good tactical powers, great courage and determination. He does not think Murray will dare to do anything but agree with everything French suggests. In any case he thinks French would not listen to Murray but rely on Wilson, which is far worse. D.H. thinks Wilson is a politician, and not a soldier, and "politician" with Douglas Haig is synonymous with crooked dealing and wrong sense of values.' This judgement is similar to that of another General, eminent as a military historian: 'There could hardly have been worse selected GHQs than those with which we began the South African War and 1914.'

But apart from errors in selection, there is the question whether officers were miscast for their actual roles. In 1912 French himself had expressed the opinion that certainly Haig and perhaps Grierson would 'always shine more and show to greater advantage as superior staff officers than as commanders'. Because of his unrivalled knowledge of the German Army and cordial relations with the French, as well as his gift for putting juniors at their ease, Grierson would have been a peculiarly good Chief of Staff for French. Yet 'when Grierson – his Chief Staff Officer at manoeuvres – had pointed out to French the impracticability of some of his proposals, he had at once been replaced by Sir Archibald Murray'. Grierson, instead, went to France as commander of an army corps. A man of full figure and sedentary habits, fifty-five years old, the combination of good living and hard work had undermined his constitution; he collapsed and died on his way to the front. If this was a great loss to the Army, it was a less immediate danger than Murray's subsequent collapse on August 26th, the critical day of Le Cateau. Worse still, Murray would recover sufficiently to think that he was functioning when actually he was still unfit. These were but two of the most prominent instances of the trouble caused by a system which brought officers to high position at an age when their energy was declining, and their susceptibility to the strain of war increasing. As a fortunate offset the enemy suffered at least as heavily from this handicap: indeed, the directing head of the German armies, Moltke, who had recently been undergoing treatment, caused alarm among his entourage in the very first days of war by his state of semi-collapse.

The other British corps commander, Haig, had taken too good care of his health to cause any such anxiety. Physically, his fitness at fifty-three was exceptional. In the South African War, his thoroughness and methodicity had made him an ideal staff officer to French; but later, when given command of a mobile column, those qualities had not proved all-sufficing. It is worth recalling that when Colonel Woolls-Sampson, 'the incomparable Intelligence officer and fighting scout', was told of Haig's appointment as column commander, he remarked: 'He's quite all right, but he's too — cautious: he will be so fixed on not giving the Boers a chance, he'll never give himself one.' Thirteen years later Woolls-Sampson's point was borne out. For the revised Official History of 1914, published after a generation has passed, has revealed that at Haig's first serious test as a corps commander he was temporarily thrown off his balance by a trifling encounter in the dark, so that he reported 'situation very critical', and repeatedly called for help – from a neighbour who was really hard pressed. It has also revealed that Haig's excessive caution on reaching the Aisne allowed the day of opportunity to slip away, and the enemy to establish their four years' tenure of the position beyond. Yet if command was not Haig's natural role, he had developed qualities which others lacked, and once the battlefront became static the conditions of warfare tended to change the role of a commander into that of a super-staff officer.

Errors of conception were to cost more than any errors of execution. Lessons of the South African War that went wider than the selection of leaders had been overlooked. Read in the light of 1914–18, the 'Evidence taken before the Royal Commission on the War in South Africa' offers astonishing proof of how professional vision may miss the wood for the trees. There is little hint, among those who were to be the leaders in the next war, that they had recognized the root problem of the future – the dominating power of fire defence and the supreme difficulty of crossing the bullet-swept zone. Sir Ian Hamilton alone gave it due emphasis, and even he was too sanguine as to the possibility of overcoming it. His proposed solution, however, was in the right direction. For he urged not only the value of exploiting surprise and infiltration tactics to nullify the advantages of the defence, but the need of heavy field artillery to support the infantry. Still more prophetically, he suggested that the infantry might be provided with 'steel shields on wheels' to enable them to cross no-man's-land and make a lodgement in the enemy's position.

Mr Amery, author of *The Times* history of the war, probed a weak spot in the prevailing European theory by arguing that superior skill now counted more than superior numbers, and that its proportionate value would increase with material progress. The same note was struck by General Baden-Powell, who urged that the way to develop it was to give officers responsibility when young – he was left to find his channel for proving this in the Boy Scout movement, and not in the Army.

Two generals, Paget and Hunter, had a vision of the value and future use of motor vehicles in war, while Haig said that, rather than mounted infantry, he would prefer infantry 'on motors'. In view of the development of the motor between 1903 and 1914 it is strange how little use of it was made at the outset of the next war – or even at the end!

But the most remarkable feature of this Royal Commission was the way that French and Haig discoursed on the paramount value of the *arme blanche*, implying that so long as the cavalry charge was maintained all would be well with the conduct of war. An equally striking underestimate of fire power was contained in Haig's forecast that 'artillery seems only likely to be really effective against raw troops'. His confident opening declaration was that 'cavalry will have a larger sphere of action in future wars'. And he went on to say: 'Besides being used before, during, and after a battle as hitherto, we must expect to see it employed strategically on much larger scale than formerly.' What a contrast there was to be between this expectation and the event! French, Germans, Russians, and Austrians certainly had unexampled masses of cavalry ready at the outbreak of war. But in the opening phase they caused more trouble to their own sides than to the enemy. From 1915 on, their effect was trivial, except as a strain on their own country's supplies: despite the relatively small number of British cavalry, forage was the largest item of supplies sent overseas, exceeding even ammunition, and thus the most dangerous factor in aggravating the submarine menace; while, by authoritative verdict, the transport trouble caused in feeding the immense number of cavalry horses was an important factor in producing Russia's collapse.

In the British Army, also, one unfortunate result of this delusion was that when the cavalry school came to the top in the years just before the war, there was the usual human tendency to penalize the careers of officers who propounded more realistic ideas, while a still larger circle were thereby induced to maintain silence. This was the greater pity because the cavalry sense of mobility was as vital a necessity as the cavalry means of mobility was decadent; and by undue emphasis on the old means the chance of re-creating the means was hindered.

But in other ways the bitter lessons of the South African War brought profit, exerting an influence which to some extent counteracted that inelasticity of mind and ritualism of method which have increased with the increasing professionalization of armies. For the progress in organization in the years before 1914, the British Army owed much to Lord Haldane,* and to him also was due the creation of a second line of partially trained citizens – the Territorial Force. Lord Roberts had pleaded for compulsory military training, but the voluntary principle was too deeply embedded in the national mind for this course to be adopted, and Haldane wisely sought to develop Britain's military effectiveness within the bounds set by traditional policy. As a result, 1914 found England with an expeditionary force of some 160,000 men, the most highly trained striking force of any country – a rapier among scythes. To maintain this at strength the old militia had been turned into a special reserve for drafting. Behind this first line stood the Territorial Force, which if only enlisted for home defence had a permanent fighting organization, unlike the amorphous volunteer force which it superseded. The British Army had no outstanding asset in war armament, but it had developed a standard of rifle-shooting unique among the world's armies.

The reforms by which the army had been brought into line with continental models had one defect, accentuated by the close relations established between the British and French General Staffs since the Entente. It induced a 'continental' habit of thought among the General Staff, and predisposed them to the role, for which their slender strength was unsuited, of fighting alongside an Allied army. This obscured the British Army's traditional employment in amphibious operations through which the mobility given by command of the sea could be exploited. A small but highly trained force striking 'out of the blue' at a

* He found an ardent assistant in Haig, whose appointment to the War Office had been strongly urged by King Edward.

vital spot can produce a strategic effect out of all proportion to its slight numbers.

The last argument brings us to a comparison of the naval situation, which turned on the balance between the fleets of Britain and Germany. Britain's sea supremacy, for long unquestioned, had in recent years been challenged by a Germany which had deduced that a powerful fleet was the key to that colonial empire which she desired as an outlet for her commerce and increasing population. This ambition was fostered, as its instrument was created, by the dangerous genius of Admiral von Tirpitz. To the spur of naval competition the British people eventually responded, determined at any cost to maintain their 'two-power' standard. If this reaction was instinctive rather than reasoned, its subconscious wisdom had a better foundation than the catchwords with which it was justified, or even than the need of defence against invasion. The industrial development of the British Isles had left them dependent on overseas supplies for food, and on the secure flow of seaborne imports and exports for industrial existence. For the navy itself this competition was a refining agency, leading to a concentration on essentials. Gunnery was developed and less value attached to polished brasswork. Warship design and armament were transformed; the 'Dreadnought' ushered in the new era of the big-gun battleship. By 1914 Britain had twenty-nine such capital ships and thirteen building, to the eighteen built and nine building, of Germany. Further, Britain's naval strength had been soundly distributed, the main concentration being in the North Sea.

More open to criticism in view of the forecasts of several naval authorities, was her comparative neglect of the potential menace of the submarine. Here German opinion was shown rather by the number building than those already in commission. It is to Germany's credit that though lacking a sea tradition, her fleet an artificial rather than a natural product, the technical skill of the German Navy made it a formidable rival to the British ship for ship, and perhaps its superior in scientific gunnery.

But in the first stage of the struggle the balance of the naval forces was to affect the issue far less than the balance on land. For a fleet suffers one inherent limitation – it is tied to the sea, and hence cannot strike direct at the hostile nation. The fundamental purpose of a navy is therefore to protect a nation's sea communications and sever those of the enemy; although victory in battle may be a necessary prelude, blockade is its ultimate purpose. And as blockade is a weapon slow to take effect, its influence could only be decisive if the armies failed to secure the speedy decision on land, upon which all counted.

In this idea of a short war lay also the reason for the comparative disregard of economic forces. Few believed that a modern nation could endure for many months the strain of a large-scale conflict. The supply of food and of funds, the supply and manufacture of munitions, these were problems that had been only studied on brief estimates. Of the belligerents, all could feed themselves save Britain and Germany, and Germany's deficit of home-grown supplies could only be serious in the event of a struggle of years. But Britain would starve in three months if her outside supplies were cut off.

In munitions and other war material Britain's industrial power was greatest of all, though conversion to war production was a necessary preliminary, and all, again, depended on the security of her sea communications. France was weak, and Russia weaker still, but the former unlike the latter could count on outside supplies so long as Britain held the seas. As Britain was the industrial pivot of the one alliance, so was Germany of the other. A great manufacturing nation, she had also a wealth of raw material, especially since the annexation of the Lorraine ironfields after the 1870 war. But the stoppage of outside supplies must be a handicap in a long war, increasing with its duration, and serious from the outset in such tropical products as rubber. Moreover, Germany's main coal and ironfields lay dangerously close to her frontier, in Silesia on the east and in Westphalia and Lorraine on the west. Thus for the Central Alliance a quick decision and an offensive war were more essential than for the Entente.

Similarly, financial resources had been calculated on a short war basis, and all the Continental Powers relied mainly on large gold reserves accumulated specially for war purposes. Britain alone had no such war chest, but she was to prove that the strength of her banking system and the wealth distributed among a great commercial people furnished the 'sinews of war' in a way that few pre-war economists had realized.

If the economic forces were neglected in the war calculations of the Powers, the psychological forces were an unexplored region, except in their purely military aspect. And even here little study had been devoted to the moral element compared with the physical element. Ardant du Picq, a soldier-philosopher who fell in the 1870 war, had stripped battle of its aura of heroic fictions, portraying the reaction of normal men in the presence of danger. Several German critics had described from experience the reality of battle morale as shown in 1870, and had deduced how tactics should be based on the ever-present and balancing elements of fear and courage. At the close of the century a French military thinker, Colonel Foch, had demonstrated how great was the influence of the moral element in the higher sphere of command, although his teaching was concerned rather with fortifying the will of the commander than with unhinging the will of the opponent. But only the surface of the subject had been penetrated. Its civil aspects were untouched, and in the opening weeks of the conflict the general misunderstanding of national psychology was to be shown in the muzzling of the press – in Britain due mainly to Kitchener, followed by the equally stupid practice of issuing *communiqués* which so veiled the truth that public opinion became distrustful of all official news and rumour was loosed on its infinitely more damaging course. The true value of wisely calculated publicity and the application of the propaganda weapon were only to be learnt after many blunders.

CHAPTER THREE

The Rival War Plans

In an historical survey the German plan must justly take priority, for not only was it the mainspring which set in motion the hands of the war clock in 1914, but it may even be said to have governed the course of the war thereafter. It is true that, from the autumn of 1914 onwards, this course outwardly seemed to be of the nature of a stupendous 'siege' of the Central Powers, an idea incompatible with the terms we have used. But the conception of the Germanic Alliance as a besieged party, although true of the economic sphere, suggests a loss of initiative which their strategy contradicts. Although the initial German plan miscarried, even in its failure it dictated the general trend of operations thereafter. Tactically, most of the fighting resembled siege operations, but the actual strategy on land long erred rather by its disregard of these tactical conditions than by its conformity with them.

The Germans were faced with the problem that the combined forces of themselves and Austria were decidedly inferior to those of France and Russia. To offset this adverse balance, however, they had a central position and the anticipation that Russia's mobilization would be too slow to allow her to exert serious pressure in the opening weeks. While this assumption might suggest a decisive blow at Russia before she was ready, it was equally probable that she would concentrate her main forces too far back for such a German blow to reach – and the experience of Napoleon was not an example to encourage an advance deep into the interior of Russia, with its vast distances and poor communications. The plan long since adopted by Germany was, therefore, to deliver a rapid offensive against France while holding the Russian advanced forces at bay; and later, when France was crushed, to deal with the Russian army. But this plan, in turn, was complicated by the great natural and artificial barriers which the French frontier offered to an invader. It was narrow, only some 150 miles across, and so afforded little room to manoeuvre or even to deploy the masses that Germany planned to launch against her foe. At the south-eastern end it abutted on Switzerland, and after a short stretch of flat country known as the Gap of Belfort the frontier ran for seventy miles along the Vosges mountains. Behind and prolonging this natural rampart ran an almost continuous fortress system, based on Epinal, Toul, Verdun, and twenty miles beyond the last-named lay not only the frontiers of Luxembourg and Belgium but the difficult Ardennes country. Apart from the strongly defended avenues of advance by Belfort and Verdun, the only feasible gap in this barrier was the Trouée de Charmes between Epinal and Toul, left open originally as a strategic trap in which the Germans could be first caught and then crushed by a French counterstroke.

Faced with such a mental and physical blank wall, the logical *military* course was to go round it – by a wide manoeuvre through Belgium. Graf Schlieffen, Chief of the German General Staff from 1890 to 1905, conceived and developed the plan, by which the French armies were to be enveloped and a rapid decision gained; and as finally formulated it came into force in 1905. To attain its object Schlieffen's plan concentrated the mass of the German forces on the right wing for a gigantic wheel and designedly took risks by reducing the left wing, facing the French frontier, to the slenderest possible size. The swinging mass, pivoting on the fortified area Metz-Thionville, was to consist of fifty-three divisions, backed up as rapidly as possible by Landwehr and Ersatz formations, while the secondary army on the left wing comprised only eight divisions. Its very weakness promised to aid the main blow in a further way, for if a French offensive pressed the left wing back towards the Rhine, the attack through Belgium on the French flank would be all the more difficult to parry. It would be like a revolving door – if a man pressed heavily on one side the other side would swing round and strike him in the back. Here lay the real subtlety of the plan, not in the mere geographical detour.

The German enveloping mass was to sweep round through Belgium and northern France and, continuing to traverse a vast arc, would wheel gradually east. With its extreme right passing south of Paris and crossing the Seine near Rouen it would then press the French back towards the Moselle, where they would be hammered in rear on the anvil formed by the Lorraine fortresses and the Swiss frontier.

Schlieffen's plan allowed ten divisions to hold the Russians in check while the French were being crushed. It is proof of his clear sight, if not of his long sight, that he counted on the intervention of Britain, and allowed for an expeditionary force of 100,000 'operating in conjunction with the French'. To him also was due the scheme for using the Landwehr and Ersatz troops in active operations and fusing the resources of the nation into the army. His dying words are reported to have been: 'It must come to a fight. Only make the right wing strong.'

Unhappily for Germany, his successor, Moltke 'the younger', lacked his moral courage while sharing his disregard of international morality. Moltke retained Schlieffen's plan, but he whittled away the essential idea. Of the nine new divisions which became available between 1905 and 1914 Moltke allotted eight to the left wing and only one to the right. True, he added another from the Russian front, but this trivial increase was purchased at a heavy price, for the Russian Army of 1914 was a more formidable menace than when Schlieffen's plan came into force. In the outcome two army corps were taken from the French theatre at the crisis of the August campaign, in order to reinforce the Eastern Front. Schlieffen's deathbed entreaty was lost on his successor.

Moltke also made a change of great political significance in the plan. Schlieffen had intended that the right wing should deploy along not only the Belgian but also the Dutch frontier, as far north as Crefeld. By crossing the strip of Dutch territory known as the 'Maastricht Appendix' it would be able to turn the flank of the Liége forts, which barred the way through the narrow Belgian gateway north of the Ardennes. He hoped that German diplomacy might secure permission for this passage through Holland, and he did not wish to violate the territory of either Belgium or Holland if he could avoid the moral reproach. For it was his calculation that the undisguised deployment there of part of his force would so alarm the French as to induce them to cross the southern frontier of Belgium and occupy the natural defensive position in the Meuse valley, south of Namur. Thereby they would provide a pretext for his own advance into neutral territory. Even should this subtle trap fail, Schlieffen calculated that he would be able to capture Liége in time to avoid any check on his main advance. And he was willing to cut his margin of time so close as to afford German statecraft the fullest chance to escape the charge of rape.

Such imaginative craft was beyond Moltke's capacity, and he decided that Liége must be taken by a *coup de main* immediately after the outbreak of war. Thus for a fancied addition to military security he deliberately invited the condemnation of neutrals, provoked Belgium to resistance, and drew the weight of Britain into the scales against his own forces. Moltke's method of 'drawing' the enemy was certainly the antithesis of Schlieffen's. And it is a glaring example of the dangers, even the military dangers, which may ensue if strategy is allowed to dominate policy.

If the fault of the final German plan was a lack of courage, that of the French plan was due to an excess. In their case, also, a miasma of confused thought seemed to creep over the leadership in the years just before the war. Since the disasters of 1870 the French Command had planned an initial defensive, based on the frontier fortresses, followed by a decisive counterstroke. To this end the great fortress system had been created and gaps like the Trouée de Charmes left to 'canalize' the invasion ready for the counter. But in the decade before 1914 a new school of thought had risen, who argued that the offensive was more in tune with French character and tradition, that the possession of the '75' – a field gun unique in mobility and rapidity of fire – made it tactically possible, and that the alliance with Russia and Britain made it strategically possible. Forgetful of the lessons of 1870 they imagined that *élan* was proof against bullets. Napoleon's much-quoted saying that 'the moral is to the physical as three to one' has much to answer for; it has led soldiers to think that a division exists between the two, whereas each is dependent on the other. Weapons without courage are ineffective, but so also are the bravest troops without sufficient weapons to protect them and their morale. Courage soon oozes when soldiers lose confidence in their weapons.

The outcome was disastrous. The new school, who found their prophet in Colonel de Grandmaison, found in General Joffre, appointed Chief of the General Staff in 1912, a lever for their designs. Under the cloak of his authority, the advocates of the *offensive à outrance* gained control of the French military machine, and, throwing aside the old doctrine, formulated the now famous, or notorious, Plan XVII. It was based on a negation of historical experience, indeed, of common-sense, and on a double miscalculation – of force and place, the latter more serious than the former. Accepting the possibility that the Germans might employ their reserve formations at the outset, the strength of the German army in the west was estimated at a possible maximum of sixty-eight infantry divisions. The Germans actually deployed the equivalent of eighty-three, counting Landwehr and Ersatz troops. But French opinion was, and continued to be, doubtful of this contingency, so much so that during the crucial days when the rival armies were concentrating and moving forward the French Intelligence counted only the forty-five active divisions in its estimates of the enemy strength – a miscalculation by half. If the plan had been framed on a miscalculation less extreme, this recognition does not condone but rather increases its fundamental falsity: for history affords no vestige of justification for a plan by which a frontal offensive was to be launched with bare equality of force against an enemy who would have the support of his fortified frontier zone, while the attackers forswore any advantage from their own.

The second miscalculation – of place – was that although the possibility of a German move through Belgium was recognized, the wideness of its sweep was utterly misjudged. The Germans were expected complaisantly to take the difficult route through the Ardennes in order that the French might conveniently smite their communications! Based on the idea of an immediate and general offensive, the plan ordained a thrust by the First and Second Armies towards the Saar into Lorraine. On their left were the Third Army opposite Metz and the Fifth Army facing the Ardennes, which were either to take up the offensive between Metz and Thionville, or, if the Germans came through Luxembourg and Belgium, to strike north-east at their flank. The Fourth Army was held in strategic reserve near the centre and two groups of reserve divisions were disposed in rear of either flank – relegation to such a passive role expressing French opinion on the capacity of reserve formations.

Britain's contingent share in this plan was settled less by calculation than by the 'Europeanization' of her military organization during the previous decade. This continental influence drew her insensibly into a tacit acceptance of the role of acting as an appendix to the French left wing, and away from her historic exploitation of the mobility given by sea power. At a council of war on August 5th, Sir John French, who was to command the expeditionary force, expressed a doubt of 'the prearranged plan', and, as an alternative, suggested its dispatch to Belgium – where it would have stiffened the Belgian resistance and threatened the flank of the wheeling German mass. Haig seems to have had a similar view. But the plan did not provide for variation, and in any case the General Staff, through Henry Wilson, had virtually pledged themselves to act in direct cooperation with the French. When the General Staffs of the two countries conducted their informal negotiations between 1905 and 1914, they were paving the way for a reversal of England's centuries-old policy for a war effort such as no Englishman had ever conceived.

Lord Kitchener, who had just been made War Minister in the emergency, had a remarkably accurate intuition of the German plan and tried to avert the danger by advocating that the expeditionary force should concentrate near Amiens, where it would be less exposed. But French was now in accord with Wilson, and his vehement support of the French plan induced Kitchener to give way – later he lamented his consent as a mistaken weakness. Kitchener, however, gave French instructions which, designed to reduce the risks, were in the issue to complicate and even to increase them. For while French's assigned purpose was 'to support, and cooperate with, the French Army', it was qualified by the somewhat contradictory statement 'that the gravest consideration will devolve upon you as to participation ... where your force may be unduly exposed ...' Further, 'you will in no case come in any sense under the orders of any Allied General'.

The smoothness and secrecy with which the expeditionary force moved to France (the main part between August 12th and 17th) was a testimony to the transport arrangements and counter-espionage measures, if still more to the shortsightedness of the Germans. Not merely did their intelligence service fail to gain news of the British expeditionary force until it was actually encountered, but the supreme Command showed little concern with its whereabouts. When Moltke was asked if he desired the Navy to interfere with the passage of the British troops, he showed no enthusiasm for the idea, saying that 'it would be indeed splendid if the Army in the west could settle with the 160,000 English at the same time as with the other enemies'. In their pedantic adherence to the principle of concentration both the General Staff and the Naval Staff ignored the importance of distraction. And each remained in its own narrow compartment, with little interest in what the other was doing and less desire to communicate its own intentions.

The General Staff's mind was fixed on the aim of a decisive battle, without a thought for the Channel ports; the detachments it made, so fateful in their effect, were for the negative purpose of protecting its own march, and not to embarrass the enemy. The Naval Staff's dominant idea was to keep the fleet concentrated in the North Sea, ready for eventualities but with little concern to influence events. Its positive action was limited to sending out a few submarines in a half-hearted manner. The idea of a landing on the English coast, or even a feint, does not seem to have been considered – although the mere possibility sufficed to detain a considerable part of Britain's military strength. Nor had the General Staff made plans for embarrassing Britain at long range by encouraging native risings. A swift victory over the main armies in the main theatre of war was the German General Staff's solution for all outside difficulties, and absolved them from thinking of war in its wider aspects.

On the Russian front, the plans of campaign were more fluid, less elaborately worked out and formulated, although they were to be as kaleidoscopic in their changes of fortune as in the western theatre. The calculable condition was geographical; the main incalculable, Russia's rate of concentration. Russian Poland was a vast tongue of country projecting from Russia proper, and flanked on three sides by German or Austrian territory. On its northern flank lay East Prussia with the Baltic Sea beyond. On its southern flank lay the Austrian province of Galicia with the Carpathian mountains to the south, guarding the approach to the plain of Hungary. On the west lay Silesia. As the Germanic border provinces were provided with a network of strategic railways whilst Poland, as well as Russia itself, had only a sparse system of communications, the Germanic Alliance enjoyed a great advantage, in power of concentration, for countering a Russian advance. But if its armies took the offensive, the farther they progressed into Poland or Russia proper the more would they lose this advantage. Hence their most profitable strategy was to lure the Russians into a position favourable for a counterstroke rather than to inaugurate an offensive themselves. The one drawback was that such a Punic strategy gave the Russians time to concentrate and set in motion their cumbrous and rusty machine.

From this arose an initial cleavage between German and Austrian opinion. Both agreed that the problem was to hold the Russians in check during the six weeks which must elapse before the Germans should have crushed France, and so could switch their forces eastwards to join the Austrians in a decisive blow against the Russians. The difference of opinion turned on the method. The Germans, intent on a decision against France, wished to leave a minimum force in the east, and only a political dislike of exposing national territory to invasion prevented them from evacuating East Prussia and standing on the Vistula line. But the Austrians, under the influence of Conrad von Hötzendorf, chief of their General Staff, were anxious to throw the Russian machine out of gear by an immediate offensive, and, as this promised to keep the Russians fully occupied while the campaign in France was being decided, Moltke fell in with this strategy.

Conrad's plan was that of an offensive northwards into Poland by two armies, protected by two more on their right, farther east. The two attacking armies would then wheel eastwards, and all four would join hands in driving the Russians back towards the Black Sea. Complementary to this plan, as originally designed, the Germans in East Prussia were to strike south-east, the two forces converging to cut off the Russian advanced forces in the Polish 'tongue'. But Moltke failed to provide sufficient German troops for this offensive thrust.

Conrad's own offensive was to be impaired by the combination of a variable state of mind with an inelastic basis of movement. The Austrian forces had been divided into three parts: 'Echelon A' (28 divisions) for deployment on the Russian front; *'Minimum Balkan'* (8 divisions) for deployment on the Serbian front; 'Echelon B' (12 divisions) for use according to circumstances. The plan thus had more adaptability, on paper, than those of other armies; unfortunately, the instrument was not equal to the intention. Conrad's desire to settle with Serbia led him to begin moving 'Echelon B' thither, despite the likelihood of Russia's intervention. Then, on July 31st, he changed his mind and decided to stop it. But 'the Chief of the Field Railways informed him that if utter confusion was to be avoided he must allow "B" to go to its original destination on the Danube frontier, and from there it could be transported to Galicia'. As a result, its withdrawal from the Danube impaired the offensive against Serbia without helping that against Russia, for which it arrived too late. Thus a conflict of purpose in the Austrian Command accentuated the ill-effects of a conflict of interests between Austria and her ally.

On the opposing side also, the desires of one ally vitally affected the strategy of the other. The Russian command, both for military and for racial motives, wished to concentrate first against Austria, while the latter was unsupported, and leave Germany alone until later, when the full strength of the Russian Army would be mobilized. But the French, anxious to relieve the German pressure against themselves, urged the Russians to deliver a simultaneous attack against Germany, and persuaded the Russians to consent to an extra offensive for which they were ready neither in numbers nor in organization. On the south-western front two pairs of two armies each were to converge on the Austrian forces in Galicia; on the north-western front two armies were to converge on the German forces in East Prussia. Russia, whose proverbial slowness and crude organization dictated a cautious strategy, was about to break with tradition and launch out on a gamble that only an army of high mobility and organization could have hoped to bring off.

When put to the test, the plans of all the military commanders would quickly collapse. At a superficial examination, the fault would seem due to divided purposes in the minds of the leaders – to their failure to maintain the principle of 'concentration' with which they had been indoctrinated. It is easy to point out how they failed in this way – many books by military experts have done so. But such a judgement is too academic. The fact that the fault was common to all sides suggests a deeper explanation. Not one of the leaders was anything but a devout upholder of the principle of concentration in theory: the trouble came when they tried to apply it to reality – to the political and tactical conditions in which strategy operates. Their failure to adapt their plans to the actual situation may be traced to the habit of mind formed in peace training; especially in war games and exercises, where battle was the ruling idea, the conventions too exclusively military, and the values too purely numerical. By treating concentration as a matter of assembling superior numbers, its dependence on the enemy's distraction and on freedom from external interference was too commonly obscured.

Peace training tended towards solutions that were idealistic rather than realistic. For war, like politics, is a series of compromises. Hence the need of adaptation should be foreseen, the power of adjustment developed, in the pre-war preparation. This was rare among the staff-trained leaders of 1914. They had been brought up on a diet of theory, supplemented by scraps of history cooked to suit the prevailing taste: not on the experience contained in real history. For this to be attainable a critical mind is the first requirement; but such a faculty was frowned on by the military tradition of the nineteenth century – although marked in many great leaders of the eighteenth century.

CHAPTER FOUR

1914 – The Clinch

The German invasion of France was designed as a methodical sweep, in which unexpected checks should not upset the timetable. The railway system in Germany had been developed under military guidance and supervision – so strict that not even a narrow-gauge line or road rail could be laid without the approval of the Chief of the General Staff. As a result the number of double lines running to the western frontier had been increased from nine to thirteen between 1870 and 1914. On August 6th the great deployment began; 550 trains a day crossed the Rhine bridges, and by the 12th the seven German armies (1,500,000 men) were ready to advance. Over the Hohenzollern bridge at Cologne a train passed about every ten minutes during the first fortnight of war. This vast railway movement was a masterpiece of organization, but when the deployment, completed on August 17th, merged into the forward march, the friction of war soon revealed weaknesses in the German military machine and its control.

To meet the case of Belgian resistance the German plan, as revised by Moltke, provided an instantly available detachment, under General von Emmich, to clear a passage through the Meuse gateway into the Belgian plain north of the Ardennes, ready for the ordered advance of the main armies concentrating behind the German frontier. The ring fortress of Liége commanded this channel of advance, but, after an initial check on August 5th, a German brigade penetrated between the forts and occupied the town. The interest of this feat is that it was due to the initiative of an attached staff officer, Ludendorff, whose name ere long was to be world famous. The forts themselves offered a stubborn resistance and forced the Germans to await the arrival of their heavy howitzers, whose destructive power was to be the first tactical surprise of the World War.

The very success of the Belgians' early resistance cloaked the weight of the main German columns and misled the Allies' Intelligence. The Belgian field army lay behind the Gette covering Brussels and, even

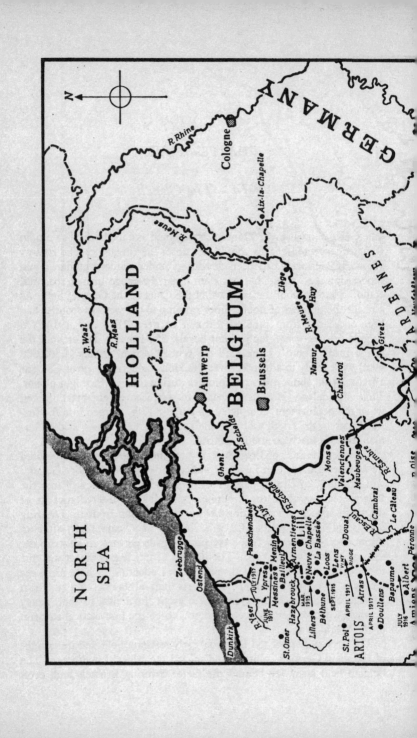

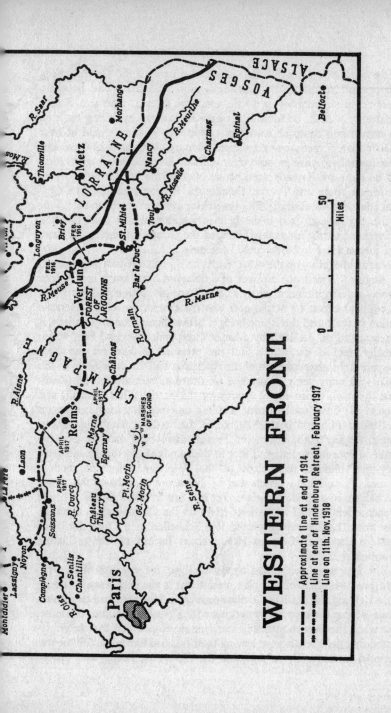

WESTERN FRONT

Approximate line at end of 1914
Line at end of Hindenburg Retreat, February 1917
Line on 11th. Nov. 1918

0   50
Miles

ALSACE
VOSGES
Belfort
R.Saar
Morhange
R.Meurthe
Charmes
Epinal
Thionville
Metz
Nancy
LORRAINE
R.Moselle
R.Mos.
Longuyon
Briey
FEB. 1916
St.Mihiel
Toul
R.Meuse
FEB. 1916
Verdun
Bar le Duc
FOREST OF ARGONNE
R.Marne
R.Ornain
CHAMPAGNE
Châlons
R.Aisne
APRIL 1917
Reims
APRIL 1917
R.Marne
Epernay
MARSHES OF ST.GOND
Pt.Morin
Gd.Morin
La Fère
Laon
APRIL 1917
R.Ourcq
Soissons
Château Thierry
R.Seine
Montdidier
Lassigny
Noyon
Compiègne
Senlis
Chantilly
R.Oise
Paris

before the Liége forts fell, the advanced guards of the German First and Second Armies were pressing against this line. The Belgians, deprived of support owing to the mistaken French plan and British conformity with it, decided to preserve their army by falling back on the entrenched camp of Antwerp – where its location would at least make it a latent menace to the German communications. The Germans, their immediate passage now clear, entered Brussels on August 20th, and on the same day appeared before Namur, the last fortress barring the Meuse route into France. Despite the Belgian resistance the German advance was abreast of its timetable; but it might have been four or five days ahead. And if the Belgian withdrawal to a flank momentarily expedited, it ultimately hindered the German progress, far more than any sacrifice in battle could have done.

Meanwhile, away on the other flank, the French offensive had opened on August 7th with the advance of a detached army corps into Upper Alsace, a move intended partly as a military distraction and partly for its political effect. Its actual goal was the destruction of the German station at Basle and the Rhine bridges below. Soon brought to a halt, it was renewed on the 19th by a larger force under General Pau, which actually reached the Rhine. But the pressure of disasters elsewhere compelled the abandonment of the enterprise and the dissolution of the force – its units being dispatched westward as reinforcements. Meantime the main thrust into Lorraine by the French First (Dubail) and Second (de Castelnau) Armies, totalling nineteen divisions, had begun on August 14th and been shattered in the battle of Morhange–Sarrebourg, August 20th, where the French discovered that the material could subdue the moral, and that in their enthusiasm for the offensive they had blinded themselves to the defensive power of modern weapons, a condition which was to throw out of balance the whole mechanism of orthodox warfare. Yet it is fair to add that this abortive French offensive had an indirect effect on the German plan, although this would hardly have occurred if a Schlieffen or a Ludendorff had been in charge at German Headquarters instead of the vacillating opportunist Moltke.

The fact that Moltke had almost doubled the strength of his left, compared with Schlieffen's plan, meant that it was unnecessarily strong for a yielding and 'enticing' defensive such as Schlieffen had conceived, while lacking the superiority necessary for a crushing counter-offensive. But when the French attack in Lorraine developed and Moltke appreciated that the French were leaving their fortified barrier behind he was tempted momentarily to postpone the right-wing sweep, and instead seek a decision in Lorraine. This impulse led him to divert thither the six newly formed Ersatz divisions that should have been used to increase the weight of his right wing. He had hardly conceived this new plan before he abandoned it and, on August 16th, reverted to Schlieffen's 'swing-door' design.

But he also told his left-wing commanders somewhat ambiguously that they must detain as many French troops as possible, and when the Crown Prince Rupprecht of Bavaria argued that he could only do this by attacking, Moltke left the decision to him. We may suspect that Rupprecht was loth to forfeit the opportunity of glory by retiring while the German Crown Prince was advancing. But nothing could have been more foolishly ambiguous than the Supreme Command's attitude. For when Rupprecht refused to refrain unless given a clear order, Moltke's deputy, Stein, said on the telephone to Krafft von Delmensingen, Rupprecht's Chief of Staff – 'No, we won't oblige you by forbidding an attack. You must take the responsibility. Make your own decision as your conscience tells you.' Conscience seems a curious basis for strategy. And when Krafft retorted, 'It is already made. We attack', Stein fatuously exclaimed, 'Not really! Then strike and God be with you.'

Thus, instead of continuing to fall back and draw the French on, Rupprecht halted his Sixth Army on the 17th, ready to accept battle. Finding the French attack slow to develop, he planned to anticipate it by one of his own. He struck on August 20th in conjunction with the Seventh Army (Heeringen) on his left, but although the French were taken by surprise and rolled back from the line Morhange–Sarrebourg, the German counterstroke had not the superiority of strength (the two armies now totalled twenty-five divisions) or of strategic position to make it decisive. Further, the attempt to envelop the French right flank by a movement through the Vosges was begun too late and failed. Thus the strategic result was merely to throw back the French on to a fortified barrier which both restored and augmented their power of resistance. And thereby they were enabled to dispatch troops to reinforce their western flank – a redistribution of strength which was to have far-reaching results in the decisive battle on the Marne.

With similar disregard of superior authority, the German Crown Prince, commanding the pivotal Fifth Army between Metz and Thionville, attacked when he had been ordered to stand on the defensive. The lack of what Colonel Foch had termed 'intellectual discipline' was to be a grave factor in Germany's failure, and for this the ambitions and jealousies of generals were to be largely responsible.

While this 'seesaw' campaign in Lorraine was in progress more decisive events were occurring to the north-west. The attack on Liége awakened Joffre to the reality of a German advance through Belgium, but not to the wideness of its sweep. And the sturdy resistance of Liége confirmed him in the opinion that the German right would pass south of it, between the Meuse and the Ardennes. Plan XVII had visualized such a move, and prepared a counter. Grasping once more at phantoms, the French Command embraced this idea so fervently that they transformed the counter into an imaginary *coup de grâce*. Their Third Army (Ruffey) and the reserve Fourth Army (de Langle de Cary) were to strike north-east through the Ardennes against the rear flank of the Germans advancing through Belgium, and thus dislocate their enveloping manoeuvre. The left wing (Fifth) Army, under Lanrezac, was moved farther to the north-west into the angle formed by the Sambre and Meuse between Givet and Charleroi. With the British Expeditionary Force coming up on its left, it was to deal with the enemy's forces north of the Meuse and to converge on the supposed German main forces in conjunction with the attack through the Ardennes. Here was a pretty picture – of the Allied pincers closing on the unconscious Germans! Curiously, the Germans had the same idea of a pincer-like manoeuvre, with roles reversed, and with better reason.

The fundamental flaw in the French plan was that the Germans had deployed twice as many troops as the French Intelligence estimated, and for a vaster enveloping movement. For information the French relied mainly on their cavalry, of which they had 100,000, but 'this enormous mass of cavalry discovered nothing of the enemy's advance ... and the French armies were everywhere surprised'. The French Third and Fourth Armies (twenty divisions), pushing blindly into the Ardennes against a German centre supposedly denuded of troops, blundered against the German Fourth and Fifth Armies (twenty-one divisions) in a fog on August 22nd, and were heavily thrown back in encounter-battles around Virton–Neufchâteau. The troops attacked blindly with the bayonet and were mown down by machine guns. Fortunately the Germans were also too vague as to the situation to exploit their opportunity.

But to the north-west the French Fifth Army (ten divisions) and the British (four divisions) had, under Joffre's orders, put their head almost into the German noose. The German masses of the First and Second Armies were closing on them from the north, and the Third Army from the east – a total of thirty-four divisions. Lanrezac alone had an inkling of the hidden menace. All along he had suspected the wideness of the

German manoeuvre, and it was through his insistence that his army had been permitted to move so far north-west. It was due to his caution in hesitating to advance across the Sambre, to the arrival of the British on his left unknown to the German Intelligence, and to the premature attack of the German Second Army, that the Allied forces fell back in time and escaped from the trap.

The Retreat to the Marne. The first four British divisions, after concentrating near Maubeuge, had moved up to Mons on August 22nd, ready to advance farther into Belgium as part of the offensive of the Allied left wing. On arrival, however, Sir John French heard that Lanrezac had been attacked on the 21st and deprived of the crossings of the Sambre. Although thus placed in an exposed forward position, he agreed to stand at Mons to cover Lanrezac's left. But next day, the 23rd, Lanrezac had word of the imminent fall of Namur and of the appearance of the German Third Army (Hausen) on his exposed right flank near Dinant, on the Meuse. In consequence, he gave orders for a retreat that night. The British, after resisting the attacks of six German divisions during the day, fell back on the 24th in conformity with their Allies. Not a moment too soon in view of the fact that the rest of the German First Army was marching still farther westward to envelop their open left flank.*

But if the British had begun to retreat later than the Allies, they continued faster and further. This less happy effect was mainly due to Sir John French's sudden revulsion of mind and emotion. He had gone forward almost too eager to fulfil the task given in Kitchener's instructions. He came back with his mind concentrated on the qualifying clause. And the change was due more to the French than to the Germans. The trouble began when Lanrezac, irritated by Joffre's blindness to the close-looming danger, vented on his newly arrived neighbour the

* Happily, the task of reducing Namur absorbed six German divisions and 500 guns from August 20th to 25th – when the last forts succumbed. This detachment, added to that already left to stand guard over Antwerp, seriously weakened the German right wing during the critical days when it fell upon and sought to overwhelm the Allied left wing in the battles of Charleroi and Mons. The delay, apparently so slight, imposed by the obsolete and neglected defences of Namur, contributed in turn to the resistance of the equally neglected French fortress of Maubeuge which did not capitulate until September 7th and detained two and a half divisions from the battlefield of the Marne. Less happily, this detachment was set free just in time to reach the Chemin des Dames ridge north of the Aisne – filling part of the gap between Kluck and Bülow (see page 95) – a few hours before the British advanced guards came up on September 12th.

indignation he could not show to his superior. This feeling was illus-
trated in the greeting which Lanrezac's Chief of Staff gave to Huguet,
who came with French to visit Lanrezac – 'At last you're here; it's not a
moment to soon. If we are beaten we shall owe it all to you!' And when
French, on being excitedly told that the Germans had reached the
Meuse at Huy, inquired what they were likely to do, Lanrezac irascibly
replied – 'Why have they come there? Oh, to fish in the river.' The
sarcasm was modified in translation. But even French's ignorance of the
French language could not prevent him understanding the impatience
and rudeness which Lanrezac showed in their discussion. Quick to
resent this, his resentment changed to alarmed disgust when he found
that the French had retired and left him isolated. Henceforward his
mind was obsessed with the idea that they had left him in the lurch, and
he thought of leaving them. The experience of the next few days
hardened his thought of retiring independently to Havre, there to
fortify himself in the peninsula with a modern version of the 'Lines of
Torres Vedras'. From this disastrous intention he was dissuaded by
Wilson's playful cajolery as well as by Kitchener's urgent and less tactful intervention, but still more by the turn of events.

The hurried recoil of the French left wing had at last awakened
Joffre to the true situation and to the utter collapse of Plan XVII. From
the wreckage he now tried to piece together a new plan. He decided to
swing back his centre and left, with Verdun as the pivot, while drawing
troops from the right in Alsace and forming a fresh Sixth Army on his
left to enable the retiring armies to return to the offensive.

His optimism, soon to wane, might have been again misplaced but
for German mistakes. The first was Moltke's folly in detaching seven
divisions to invest Maubeuge and Givet and watch Antwerp, instead of
using Landwehr and Ersatz troops as Schlieffen had intended. More
ominous still was his decision on August 25th to send four divisions to
check the Russian advance in East Prussia. These also were taken from
the right wing (actually from the force besieging Namur), and the excuse afterwards given was that the German Command thought that the
decisive victory had already been won! Further, the German Command lost touch with the advancing armies* and the movements of these
became disjointed.

---

* This vital breakdown was essentially due to the failure of the German
higher command to grasp the importance of good communication. The Chief
of the Field Telegraphs was not even consulted as to the location of the
Supreme Command. And no attempt was made to utilize the many trained
operators available in the German civil telegraph and telephone service. The

The British II Corps stand at Le Cateau, made by Smith-Dorrien against his superior's wish, and Lanrezac's riposte at Guise, in which French forbade his I Corps to help, were also factors in checking the German enveloping wing, and each had still greater indirect effects. For Le Cateau apparently convinced the German First Army commander, Kluck, that the British Army could be wiped from the slate, and Guise led Bülow (Second Army) to call on Kluck for support, whereupon Kluck wheeled inwards, thinking to roll up the French left. The idea of a Sedan was an obsession with the Germans, and led them to pluck the fruit before it was ripe. This premature wheel before Paris had been reached was an abandonment of the Schlieffen plan, and exposed the German right to a counter-envelopment.

This rash movement was in progress when Moltke also sacrificed the conception of Schlieffen to the dream of Sedan – in a different sector. His centre and left were ordered to close like pincers round either side of Verdun, while the right wing was to turn outwards and face Paris as a shield to these pincers. This sudden reversal of direction and inversion of role was akin to the folly of a driver who jams on his brakes and slews his front wheels hard round on a greasy road. One further factor must be mentioned, perhaps the most significant of all: the Germans had advanced so rapidly, outrunning their timetable, that their supplies failed to keep pace, so that the fatigue of the troops was increased by hunger.* Indeed, when the chance of battle came, their fighting power was practically numbed by physical exhaustion – a condition much aggravated by the thorough demolitions which the French had carried out as they fell back. Thus, in sum, so much grit had worked into the German machine that a slight jar would suffice to cause its breakdown. This was delivered in the battle of the Marne.

German Official History says that, as the advance proceeded 'Practically nothing was done to extend without delay the inadequate communications between Luxembourg and the right wing of the armies, or to improve them by making use of the various supplementary technical means of communication: wireless, cable, motors, aeroplanes.' Moreover, the cavalry leading the advance had shown no discrimination, and had 'recklessly destroyed both lines and instruments'.

* In one typical regimental history it is mentioned that, in order to march fast, the field kitchens had been left behind, and that there was no issue of bread for four days. The troops had to forage for what could be found in a country exhausted of supplies. And it is not surprising that on reaching the Marne the men were dead-beat, when a man went forty-eight hours on 'one piece of bread – one cup of soup – one cup of coffee – unripe fruit and a raw turnip'.

The Tide Turns. The opportunity was perceived, not by Joffre, who had ordered a continuance of the retreat, but by Galliéni, the Military Governor of Paris, where the newly formed Sixth Army had assembled in shelter. On September 3rd Galliéni realized the meaning of Kluck's wheel inwards, directed the Sixth Army (Maunoury) to be ready to strike at the exposed German right flank, and the next day with difficulty won Joffre's sanction. Once convinced, Joffre acted with decision. The whole left wing was ordered to turn about and return to a general offensive beginning on September 6th. Maunoury was already off the mark on the 5th and, as his pressure developed on the German's sensitive flank, Kluck was constrained to draw off first one part and then the remaining part of his army to support his threatened flank guard. Thereby a thirty-mile gap was created between Kluck's and Bülow's armies, a gap covered only by a screen of cavalry. Kluck was emboldened to take the risk because of the rapid retreat of the British opposite, and still with their backs to, this gaping sector. Even on the 5th, when the French on either flank were turning about, the British continued a further day's march to the south. But in this 'disappearance' lay the unintentional cause of victory. For when the British retraced their steps, it was the report of their columns advancing into the gap which, on September 9th, led Bülow to order the retreat of his army. The superficial advantage which Kluck's First Army, already isolated by its own act, had gained over Maunoury was thereby nullified, and it fell back the same day. By the 11th the retreat had extended, independently or under orders from Moltke, to all the German armies.

The attempt at a partial envelopment, pivoting on Verdun, had already failed, the jaw formed by the Sixth and Seventh Armies merely breaking its teeth on the defences of the French eastern frontier. The attack by Rupprecht's Sixth Army on the Grand Couronné, covering Nancy, was a particularly costly failure. It is difficult to see how the German Command could have reasonably pinned their faith on achieving as an improvised expedient the very task which, in cool calculation before the war, had appeared so hopeless as to lead them to take the momentous decision to advance through Belgium as the only feasible alternative.

Thus, in sum, the battle of the Marne was decided by a jar and a crack. The jar administered by Maunoury's attack on the German right flank causing a crack in a weak joint of the German line, and the penetration of this physical crack in turn producing a moral crack in the German Command.

The result was a strategic but not a tactical defeat and the German right wing was able to reknit and stand firmly on the line of the Aisne. That the Allies were not able to draw greater advantage from their victory was due in part to the comparative weakness of Maunoury's flank attack, and in part to the failure of the British and the French Fifth Army (now under Franchet d'Esperey) to drive rapidly through the gap while it was open. Their direction of advance was across a region intersected by frequent rivers and this handicap was intensified by a want of impulsion on the part of their chiefs – each politely looking to his neighbour and, timorously, to his own flanks. Their feelings can best be described by the apt verse:

> Lord Chatham with his sword undrawn
> Kept waiting for Sir Richard Strachan:
> Sir Richard, longing to be at 'em,
> Kept waiting too – for whom? Lord Chatham.

It seems, too, that greater results might have come if more effort had been made, as Gallièni urged, to strike at the German rear flank instead of the front, and to direct reinforcements to the north-west of Paris for this purpose. This view is strengthened by the sensitiveness shown by the German Command to reports of landings on the Belgian coast, which might threaten their communications. The alarm caused by these reports had even led the German Command to contemplate a withdrawal of their right wing before the battle of the Marne was launched. When the moral effect of these phantom forces is weighed with the material effect – the detention of German forces in Belgium – caused by fears of a Belgian sortie from Antwerp, the balance of judgement would seem to turn heavily in favour of the alternative which French had tentatively suggested. By it the British Expeditionary Force might have had not merely an indirect but a direct influence on the struggle, and might have made the issue not merely negatively but positively decisive.

But, considering the battle of the Marne as it shaped, the fact that twenty-seven Allied divisions were pitted against thirteen German divisions on the decisive flank is evidence, first, of how completely Moltke had lapsed from Schlieffen's intention; second, of how well Joffre had reshuffled his forces under severe pressure; third, of how such a large balance afforded scope for a wider envelopment than was actually attempted.

The frontal pursuit was checked on the Aisne before Joffre, on

September 17th, seeing that Maunoury's attempts to overlap the German flank were ineffectual, decided to form a fresh army under de Castelnau for a manoeuvre *round and behind* the German flank. By then the German armies had recovered cohesion, and the German Command was expecting and ready to meet such a manoeuvre, now the obvious course. The Allied chiefs, however, if cautious in action were incautious in speculation. Critics may complain that they were not sufficiently ingenious, but they were certainly ingenuous. Wilson and Berthelot, the guiding brains of French and Joffre, were discussing on September 12th the probable date when they would cross the German frontier. Wilson modestly estimated it at four weeks hence; Berthelot thought that he was pessimistic and reckoned on reaching the frontier a week earlier.

Flux and Stagnation. Unhappily for their calculations, on the Aisne was re-emphasized the preponderant power of defence over attack, primitive as were the trench lines compared with those of later years. Then followed, as the only alternative, the successive attempts of either side to overlap and envelop the other's western flank, a phase known popularly, but inaccurately, as the 'race to the sea'. This common design brought out what was to be a new and dominating strategical feature – the lateral switching of reserves by railway from one part of the front to another. Before it could reach its logical and lateral conclusion, a new factor intervened. Antwerp, with the Belgian Field Army, was still a thorn in the German side, and Falkenhayn, who had succeeded Moltke on September 14th, determined to reduce it while a German cavalry force swept across to the Belgian coast as an extension of the enveloping wing in France. One of the most amazing features, and blunders, of the war on the German side is that while the Allied armies were in full retreat, Moltke had made no attempt to secure the Channel ports, which lay at his mercy. The British had evacuated Calais, Boulogne and the whole coast as far as Havre; even transferred their base to St Nazaire on the Bay of Biscay, a step which not only revealed the measure of their pessimism but delayed the arrival of the reinforcing 6th Division until the German front had hardened on the Aisne. And, during the Allied retreat, German Uhlans had roamed at will over the north-west of France, settled down in Amiens as if they were permanent lodgers, yet left the essential ports in tranquil isolation. The Supreme Command was so mesmerized by its Clausewitzian dogma – 'We have only one means in war: the battle' – that it could see no purpose in securing the spoils before it had won the 'decisive battle'. A month later the Germans were to sacrifice tens of thousands of their men in the abortive effort to gain what they could have secured initially without cost.

We must pause here to pick up the thread of operations in Belgium from the moment when the Belgian Field Army fell back to Antwerp, divergently from the main line of operations. On August 24th the Belgians began a sortie against the rear of the German right wing to ease the pressure on the British and French left wing, then engaged in the opening battle at Mons and along the Sambre. The sortie was broken off on the 25th when news came of the Franco-British retreat into France, but the pressure of the Belgian Army (six divisions) led the Germans to detach four reserve divisions, besides three Landwehr brigades, to hold it in check. On September 7th the Belgian Command learnt that the Germans were dispatching part of this force to the front in France; in consequence King Albert launched a fresh sortie on September 9th – the crucial day of the battle on the Marne. The action was taken unsolicited by Joffre, who seems to have shown curiously little interest in possibilities outside his immediate battle zone. The sortie led the Germans to cancel the dispatch of one division and to delay that of two others to France, but the Belgians were soon thrown back. Nevertheless the news of it seems to have had a distinct moral effect on the German Command, coinciding as it did with the initiation of the retreat of their First and Second Armies from the Marne. And the unpleasant reminder that Antwerp lay menacingly close to their communications induced the Germans to undertake, preliminary to any fresh attempt at a decisive battle, the reduction of the fortress and the seizure of potential English landing places along the Belgian coast.

The menace to Britain, if the Channel ports fell into German hands, was obvious. It is a strange reflection that, inverting the German mistake, the British command should hitherto have neglected to guard against the danger, although the First Lord of the Admiralty, Winston Churchill, had urged the necessity even before the battle of the Marne. When the German guns began the bombardment of Antwerp on September 28th England awakened, and gave belated recognition to Churchill's strategic insight. He was allowed to send a brigade of marines and two newly formed brigades of naval volunteers to reinforce the defenders, while the Regular 7th Division and 3rd Cavalry Division, under Rawlinson, were landed at Ostend and Zeebrugge for an overland move to raise the siege. Eleven Territorial divisions were available in England, but, in contrast to the German attitude, Kitchener considered them still unfitted for an active role. The meagre reinforcement delayed, but could not prevent, the capitulation of Antwerp, October

10th, and Rawlinson's relieving force was too late to do more than cover the escape of the Belgian Field Army down the Flanders coast.

Yet, viewed in the perspective of history, this first and last effort in the west to make use of Britain's amphibious power applied a brake to the German advance down the coast which just stopped their second attempt to gain a decision in the west. It gained time for the arrival of the main British force, transferred from the Aisne to the new left of the Allied line, and if their heroic defence at Ypres, aided by the French and Belgians along the Yser to the sea, was the human barrier to the Germans, it succeeded by so narrow a margin that the Antwerp expedition must be adjudged the saving factor.

How had the main battleground come to be shifted from France to Flanders? The month following the battle of the Marne had been marked by an extremely obvious series of attempts by each side to turn the opponent's western flank. On the German side this pursuit of an opening was soon replaced by a subtler plan, but the French persevered with a straightforward obstinacy curiously akin to that of their original plan. By September 24th, de Castelnau's outflanking attempt had come to a stop on the Somme. Next, a newly formed Tenth Army, under de Maudhuy, tried a little farther north, beginning on October 2nd, but instead of being able to pass round the German flank soon found itself struggling desperately to hold Arras. The British Expeditionary Force was then in course of transfer northwards from the Aisne, in order to shorten its communications with England, and Joffre determined to use it as part of a third effort to turn the German flank. To coordinate this new manoeuvre he appointed General Foch as his deputy in the north.

Foch continued Joffre's efforts to induce the Belgians to join this wheeling mass, but King Albert with more caution, or more realism, declined to abandon the coastal district for an advance inland that he considered rash. It was. For on October 14th, four days after the fall of Antwerp, Falkenhayn planned a strategic trap for the next Allied outflanking manoeuvre which he foresaw would follow. One army, composed of troops transferred from Lorraine, was to hold the expected Allied offensive in check while another, composed of troops released by the fall of Antwerp and of four newly raised corps, was to sweep down the Belgian coast and crush in the flank of the attacking Allies. He even held back the troops pursuing the Belgians in order not to alarm the Allied Command prematurely.

Meanwhile the new Allied advance was developing piecemeal, as corps detrained from the south and swung eastwards to form a progressively extended 'scythe'. The British Expeditionary Force, now three corps* strong, deployed in turn between La Bassée and Ypres – where it effected a junction with Rawlinson's force. Beyond it the embryo of a new French Eighth Army was taking shape, and the Belgian continued the line along the Yser to the sea. Although the British right and centre corps had already been held up, Sir John French, discounting even the underestimate of the German strength furnished by his Intelligence, ordered his left corps (Haig) to begin the offensive from Ypres towards Bruges. The effort was still-born, for it coincided with the opening of the German offensive, on October 20th, but for a day or two Sir John French persisted in the belief that he was attacking while his troops were barely holding their ground.† When enlightenment came he swung to the other extreme and anxiously urged the construction of a huge entrenched camp near Boulogne 'to take the whole Expeditionary Force'. But his recurrent desire to retreat was overborne by the greater will-power, and perhaps the more consistent self-delusion of Foch, who by flattering deference, as well as forceful personality, had now gained a strong influence over French. And French's regard was increased when Foch let him know privately that Kitchener had proposed – in imagined privacy – to replace him by Sir Ian Hamilton. Too often in this war did the leaders fight each other while the troops fought the foe.

The failure of the higher commanders to grasp the situation left the real handling of the battle to Haig and his divisional commanders. And

* At this time a corps consisted of two divisions, although later of three or even four divisions.

† One cause of French's susceptibility to delusions is suggested in General Gough's record of a conversation with him shortly after the battle – when further experience should have opened his eyes – 'He thought the war would be over in three months, and that Germany could not bear the strain longer ... This seems to show that with French the wish is father to the thought, and that the thought is not the child of the careful consideration of the facts, however unpleasant, as it should be in all great men. It seems to me also to show, to some extent, his failing energy. He does not want to do any more, he does not want to be called on to make further exertions of either intellect or will-power. He hopes it is going to be ended by Russia while we remain passive here. And so his hopes become his thoughts.' Another cause lay in his physical unfitness. French, who was sixty-two, had just suffered from a severe heart attack, and was under doctor's orders to go carefully. Murray, his chief of staff, had collapsed on the critical day of Le Cateau early in the retreat from Mons. Grierson, the original commander of the II Corps, had died suddenly on the way out to France. Such facts suggest the dangers of a system of promotion which brought men to the top at a comparatively advanced age.

they for want of reserves could do little more than cement the crumbling parts of the front, by scraping reserves from other parts and encourage the exhausted but indomitable troops to hold on. Thus Ypres was essentially, like Inkerman, a 'soldiers' battle'. Already, since the 18th, the Belgians on the Yser had suffered growing pressure which threatened a disaster that was ultimately averted, by the end of the month, through the opening of the sluices and the flooding of the coastal area. At Ypres the crisis came later and was repeated, October 31st and November 11th marking the turning points of the struggle. That the Allied line, though battered and terribly strained, was in the end unbroken was due to the dogged resistance of the British and the timely arrival of French reinforcements.

This defence of Ypres is in a dual sense the supreme memorial to the British Regular Army, for here its officers and men showed the inestimable value of the disciplined morale and unique standard of musketry which were the fruit of long training, and here was their tombstone. 'From failing hands they threw the torch' to the 'New Armies' rising in England to the call of country. With the Continental Powers the merging of normal into national armies was the natural product of their system of universal service. But with Britain it was revolution, not evolution. With a supreme flash of vision Kitchener had grasped, in contrast to Governments and General Staffs alike, the probable duration of the struggle. More questionably, he decided that it meant the abandonment of Britain's traditional strategy of semi-detachment, and, donning the continental habit of thought, took the view that Britain could only exercise a decisive influence through the creation of mass armies. The people of Britain responded to his call to arms, and poured into the recruiting stations. By the end of the year nearly 1,000,000 men had enlisted, and the British Empire had altogether 2,000,000 under arms.

Having decided on this vast expansion, Kitchener chose to build a new framework rather than to use the existing Territorial foundation. It is fair to point out that the Territorial Force was enlisted for home defence and that, initially, its members' acceptance of a wider role was voluntary. But the duplication of forces and of organization was undoubtedly a source of delay and waste of effort. Kitchener has also been reproached for his reluctance to replace the voluntary system by conscription, but this criticism overlooks how deeply rooted was the voluntary system in British institutions, and the slowness with which lasting changes can be effected in them. If Kitchener's method was characteristic of the man, it was characteristic of England. If it was unmethodical, it was calculated to impress most vividly on the British people the gulf between their 'gladiatorial' wars of the past and the national war to which they were committed. It took even longer to impress the British military mind, as represented by General Headquarters in France. Henry Wilson wrote that Kitchener's 'ridiculous and preposterous army of twenty-five corps is the laughing stock of every soldier in Europe ... under no circumstances could these mobs take the field for two years. Then what is the use of them?' For by his calculation the British Army was almost due to arrive in Berlin.

While a psychological landmark, the battle of Ypres is also a military landmark. For, with the repulse of the German attempt to break through, the trench barrier was consolidated from the Swiss frontier to the sea. The power of modern defence had triumphed over attack, and stalemate ensued. The military history of the Franco-British Alliance during the next four years is a story of the attempts to upset this deadlock, either by forcing the barrier or by haphazardly finding a way round.

On the Eastern Front, however, the greater distances and the greater differences between the equipment of the armies ensured a fluidity which was lacking in the west. Trench lines might form, but they were no more than a hard crust covering a liquid expanse. To break the crust was not difficult, and, once it was broken, mobile operations of the old style became possible. This freedom of action was denied to the Western Powers, but Germany, because of her central position, had an alternative choice, and from November, 1914, onwards, Falkenhayn adopted, although for his own part unwillingly, a defensive in France while seeking to cripple the power of Russia.

The Russian Front. The opening encounters in the east had been marked by rapid changes of fortune rather than by any decisive advantage. The Austrian Command had detached part of their strength in an abortive attempt to crush Serbia. And their plan for an initial offensive to cut off the Polish 'tongue' was further crippled by the fact that the German part of the pincers did not operate. It was indeed being menaced by a Russian pair of pincers instead, for the Russian Commander-in-Chief, the Grand Duke Nicholas, had urged his First and Second Armies to invade East Prussia without waiting to complete their concentration, in order to ease the pressure on his French Allies. As the Russians had more than a two-to-one superiority, a combined attack had every chance of crushing the Germans between the two armies. On August 17th, Rennenkampf's First Army (six and a half divisions and five cavalry divisions) crossed the East Prussian frontier,

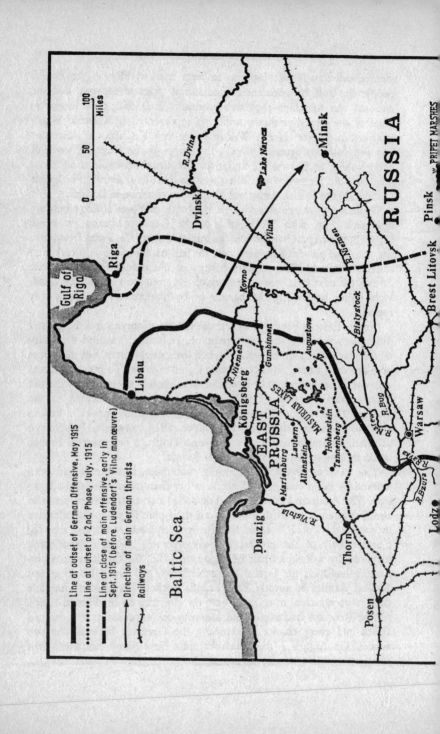

Baltic Sea

Gulf of Riga

RUSSIA

Line at outset of German Offensive, May 1915
Line at outset of 2nd. Phase, July, 1915
Line at close of main offensive, early in
Sept. 1915 (before Ludendorf's Vilna manœuvre)
Direction of main German thrusts
Railways

EAST PRUSSIA

MASURIAN LAKES

Danzig

Königsberg

Marienburg

Allenstein

Lautern

Hohenstein

Tannenberg

Thorn

Posen

Lodz

Warsaw

Brest Litovsk

Pinsk

PRIPET MARSHES

Minsk

Vilna

Kovno

Riga

Libau

Dvinsk

R.Dvina

Lake Narocz

R.Niemen

Gumbinnen

Augustova

Bialystock

R.Niemen

R.Narew

R.Bug

R.Vistula

R.Bzura

R.Raba

0   50   100
Miles

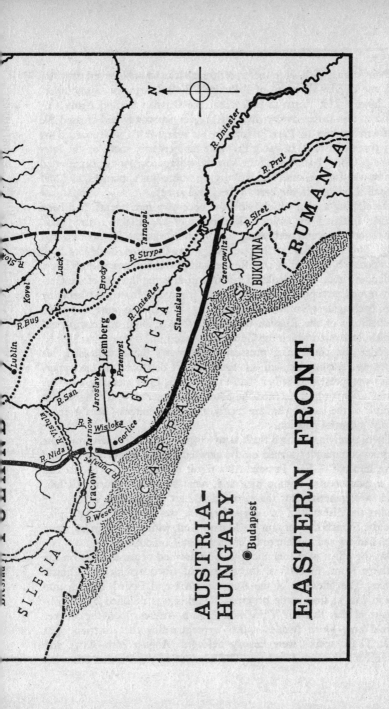

and on August 19th–20th met and threw back the bulk (seven divisions and one cavalry division) of Prittwitz's Eighth Army at Gumbinnen. On August 21st Prittwitz heard that the Russian Second Army (ten divisions and three cavalry divisions) under Samsonov had crossed the southern frontier of East Prussia, in his rear, which was guarded by only three divisions. In panic Prittwitz momentarily spoke on the telephone of falling back behind the Vistula, whereupon Moltke superseded him by a retired general, Hindenburg, to whom was appointed, as Chief of Staff, Ludendorff, the hero of the Liége attack.

Developing a plan which, with the necessary movements, had been already initiated by Colonel Hoffmann of the Eighth Army staff, Ludendorff concentrated some six divisions against Samsonov's left wing. This force, inferior in strength to the Russians, could not have been decisive, but finding that Rennenkampf was still near Gumbinnen, Ludendorff took the calculated risk of withdrawing the rest of the German troops, except the cavalry screen, from that front, and bringing them back against Samsonov's right wing. This daring move was aided by the folly of the Russian commanders in sending out unciphered wireless orders, to which the Germans listened in.

Under the converging pressure Samsonov's flanks collapsed, his centre was surrounded, and his army almost destroyed. If the opportunity was presented rather than created, this brief campaign and its sequel, afterwards christened the battle of Tannenberg, is a significant example of the use of what are technically called 'interior lines' – more simply, a central position.

Then, receiving his two fresh army corps from the French front, the German commander turned on the slow advancing Rennenkampf, and drove him out of East Prussia. As a result of these battles Russia had lost a quarter of a million men and, what she could afford still less, much war material. But the invasion of East Prussia had at least, by causing the dispatch of two corps from the west, helped to make possible the French recovery on the Marne. And, with peculiar irony, these corps had arrived too late to be of service at Tannenberg.

But the effect of Tannenberg was diminished because, away on the southern front, in Galicia, the scales had tilted against the Central Powers. The offensive of the Austrian First and Fourth Armies into Poland had at first made progress, but this was nullified by the onslaught of the Russian Third and Eighth Armies upon the weaker Second and Third Armies which were guarding the Austrian right flank. These armies were heavily defeated (August 26th–30th), and driven back through Lemberg. The advance of the Russian left wing thus threatened the rear of the victorious Austrian left wing. Conrad tried to swing part of his left round, in turn, against the Russian flank, but this blow was parried. And then, caught, with his forces disorganized, by the renewed advance of the Russian right wing, he was forced on September 11th to extricate himself by a general retreat, falling back almost to Cracow by the end of September. Austria's plight compelled the Germans to send aid, and the bulk of the force in East Prussia was formed into a new Ninth Army and switched south to the south-west corner of Poland, whence it advanced on Warsaw in combination with a renewed Austrian offensive. But the Russians were now approaching the full tide of their mobilized strength; regrouping their forces and counter-attacking, they drove back the advance and followed it up by a powerful effort to invade Silesia.

The Grand Duke Nicholas formed a huge phalanx of seven armies – three in the van and two protecting either flank. A further army, the Tenth, had invaded the eastern corner of East Prussia and was engaging the weak German forces there. Allied hopes rose high as the much-heralded Russian 'steamroller', of sixty massed divisions, began its ponderous advance. To counter it the German eastern front was placed under Hindenburg, for whom Ludendorff and Hoffmann devised a masterstroke, based on the system of lateral railways inside the German frontier, and also on a means of knowledge which to a large extent dispersed the fog of war on their side. For the continued interception of the wireless messages sent out by the Russian General Staff gave the German leaders 'a clear picture of how the enemy viewed the situation and what he intended to do'. Superior knowledge proved a compensation for inferior strength, as well as an invaluable insurance on behalf of audacity.

The Ninth Army, retreating before the advancing Russians, slowed them down by a systematic destruction of the scanty communications in Poland. On reaching its own frontier unpressed, it was first switched northwards to the Posen–Thorn area, and then thrust south-east, on November 11th – with its left flank on the Vistula – against the joint between the two armies guarding the Russian right flank.

The wedge, driven in by Ludendorff's mallet, sundered the two armies, forced the First back on Warsaw and almost effected another Tannenberg against the Second, which was nearly surrounded at Lodz, when the Fifth Army from the van turned back to its rescue. As a result, part of the German enveloping force almost suffered the fate planned for the Russians, but managed to cut its way through to the main body. If the Germans were balked of decisive tactical success this manoeuvre had been a classic example of how a relatively small force, by using its mobility to strike at a vital point, can paralyse the advance of an enemy several times its strength. The Russian 'steamroller' was thrown out of gear, and never again did it threaten German soil.

Within a week, four new German army corps arrived from the Western Front, where the Ypres attack had now ended in failure, and although too late to clinch the missed chance of a decisive victory, Ludendorff was able to use them in pressing the Russians back by December 15th to the Bzura–Ravka river line in front of Warsaw. This setback and the drying up of his munition supplies decided the Grand Duke Nicholas to break off the seesaw fighting still in progress near Cracow, and fall back on winter trench lines along the Nida and Dunajec rivers, leaving the end of the Polish 'tongue' in the hands of the enemy. Thus, on the east as on the west, the trench stalemate had settled in, but the crust was less firm, and the Russians had drained their stock of munitions to an extent that their poorly industrialized country could not make good.

The Grip on the Seas. We deal thirdly with the operations at sea, which actually occurred first in chronological order. The reason is that sea power only came to exert a dominant, eventually the dominant, influence on the war after the initial plans on land had miscarried. If the quick decision expected by the military leaders had been reached, it is questionable whether sea power could have affected the issue. How narrowly Germany missed decisive victory, and by what a combination of hardly conceivable blunders, is in the light of history now clear. While it is possible that Britain could, and would, have carried on the war unaided, we need to remember that in August, 1914, the condition was still that of a professional war with popular backing rather than a truly national war; that British intervention was still regarded as a chivalrous effort to succour violated Belgium and challenged France rather than as a life and death struggle for Britain's existence. And when a friend lies prone in a tiger's claws it is mistaken friendship to engage in a tug-of-war for the fragments if there is any chance of enticing the tiger from his prey.

But fortunately, in 1914, the tiger was held at bay and, with this breathing space gained, Britain had the opportunity to exert her traditional weapon – sea power. Its effect on the war was akin not to a lightning flash, striking down an opponent suddenly, but to a steady radiation of heat, invigorating to those it was used in aid of, and drying up the resources of the enemy.

But if its effect was extended and cumulative, its application was instantaneous, comparable almost to turning on an electric switch. This simple act, yet perhaps the most decisive of the war, took place before the actual outbreak – on July 29th when at seven o'clock in the morning that greater Armada, the British Grand Fleet, sailed from Portland for its war station at Scapa Flow. Few eyes saw its passage, fewer minds knew its destination in those northerly Orkney Isles controlling the passage between North Britain and Norway, but from that moment Germany's arteries were subjected to an invisible pressure which never relaxed until on November 21st, 1918, the German fleet arrived in those same northern waters to hand itself into the custody of a force of whom it had seen no more than a few fleeting glimpses during four and a half years of intangible struggle.

The fundamental cause of this unprecedented type of conflict lay in the recent development of new weapons, the mine and the submarine, which reproduced in naval warfare that same predominance of defensive over offensive power which was the key factor on land. The immediate cause, however, was the strategy adopted by Germany's Naval Command, partly through a miscalculation of Britain's probable strategy. Appreciating their own inferiority to the British fleet as well as the impossibility of a surprise blow in face of its preparedness, and believing that their enemy was obsessed with the Nelsonian tradition of seeking battle, the German Command adopted a Fabian strategy. They aimed to refuse conflict until their minelayers and submarines had weakened the strength of the British Navy, until the strain of a close blockade had begun to tell on the superior fleet, and perhaps provided the chance of a surprise stroke, and until the conquest of Britain's Allies on land had made her position more difficult.

The plan had at least a sound geographical basis, for the nature and configuration of the German coast lent itself to this strategy. The short North Sea coastline was heavily indented, the estuaries a maze of difficult channels, and screened by a fringe of islands – of which Heligoland formed a strongly fortified shield to the naval bases at Wilhelmshaven, Bremerhaven and Cuxhaven. Best of all, from the estuary of the Elbe there was a back door into the Baltic Sea, the Kiel Canal. By this the naval forces in the Baltic could be rapidly reinforced, while an enemy advance into that land-locked sea was not only hampered by the neutral possession of its approaches but could be imperilled by submarine and destroyer attack while passing through the narrow channels between the Danish islands. The natural defensive power of Germany's sea frontiers made attack almost impossible, and conversely gave her an excellent base for raiding operations – save for the geographical handicap that the coastline of Great Britain, like a vast breakwater, narrowed the exit for operations on the outer seas.

The one obvious defect of this Fabian strategy was that it involved the immediate abandonment of Germany's foreign trade and reduced the possibility of her interference with the sea-borne supplies of Britain and her Allies. Moreover, the German plan of progressive attrition was vitiated by the strategy adopted by the British Admiralty, which abandoned the direct doctrine of seeking out the enemy for the indirect doctrine of 'the fleet in being'. Realizing how the mine and submarine, combined with Germany's natural advantages, had made a close blockade hazardous, the Admiralty adopted a strategy of distant surveillance, keeping the battlefleet in a position which commanded the North Sea and in instant readiness for action if the enemy appeared, and using the light craft for closer, but not close observation. This strategy was not as passive as it seemed to a critical public, eagerly expecting a new Trafalgar. It appreciated that Britain's general command of the sea was the pivot of the Allied cause, and that to hazard it by exposure to uncompensated losses was the negation of this supreme requirement. Therefore, while desiring battle and being ready for it, the Admiralty quietly set about its primary duties of maintaining the security of the ocean routes, dealing with the sporadic threats to those routes, and, thirdly, ensuring the safe passage to France of the British Expeditionary Force.

The idea of economic pressure exercised by sea power was still in embryo. Not until a later phase did it crystallize into a formal doctrine, and the term 'blockade' assume a new and wider definition. The attack on sea-borne commerce was deep rooted in the traditions of the British Navy, and thus the transition to an indirect attack on the life of the enemy nation – her supplies of food and raw material – was an almost imperceptible progress. When this pressure was exercised against herself in a novel form and by a new weapon – the submarine – it was human, if illogical, that she should decry it as an atrocity. It was not easy for a conservative mind to realize that with the transition from a war of government policies into a war of peoples, intoxicated with Clausewitzian catch-phrases about a 'fight to the finish', the indefinite code of military chivalry must be submerged by the primitive instincts let loose. But in 1914 this 'absolute' war was still only a theory, and had little influence on the opening operations.

The history of the naval struggle must be dated from July 26th, 1914, when the Admiralty, in view of the clouded international situation, sent orders to the fleet assembled for review at Portland not to disperse. If the review was a happy chance the use made of it was one of the decisive acts and wisest judgements of the war, for while free from any of the provocation of an army mobilization, it placed Britain in automatic control of the situation at sea. It was followed, on July 29th, by the unnoticed sailing of the fleet for its war stations in the North Sea, and warning telegrams to all squadrons abroad. To students of war and politics the lesson should not be lost for, whatever its other limitations, a professional force has this power of unprovocative readiness which a national force inevitably lacks. 'Mobilization' is a threat, creating an atmosphere in which peaceful argument withers and dies. Between negotiations and mobilization there is a gulf, between mobilization and war an imperceptible seam, and the act of any irresponsible man can draw a nation across it.

Admiral Jellicoe, the new commander of the Grand Fleet, had one initial weakness to contend with; his base at Scapa was without defences against torpedo attack, and the fortified base being prepared at Rosyth was still incomplete. The historic concentration of British sea power had been on the Channel coast, where lay the best-prepared and defended harbours, and the Government had been slow to provide funds for bases on the North Sea to accompany the change in the concentration areas.

The danger compelled him to take his fleet west of the Orkneys, although it came down as far as the Forth during the transport to France of the Expeditionary Force – which was directly protected by the older battleships of the Channel Fleet, and by a layered system of patrols in the southern waters of the North Sea. The safe passage of the Expeditionary Force was the first direct achievement of the Navy. The next followed on August 29th when Beatty's battle-cruiser squadron and Tyrwhitt's destroyer flotillas made a swoop into the Bight of Heligoland, sank several German light cruisers, and achieved the much greater indirect effect of confirming the Germans in their strictly defensive strategy – not an unmixed blessing, for it led them to concentrate on the development of submarine attack. Apart from this engagement the story of 1914 in the North Sea is a record of unceasing vigilance on the one side; of minor submarine and minelaying successes and losses, on the other.

The war in the Mediterranean opened with a mistake that was to have far-reaching political consequences. Two of Germany's fastest ships were there, the battle cruiser *Goeben* and the light cruiser *Breslau*, and received orders from Berlin to steer for Constantinople. They evaded the British efforts made to cut them off, partly owing to inelasticity in applying the Admiralty instructions.

On the high seas the chase was more prolonged. Germany had not been allowed time to send out commerce-destroyers from home waters, but for some months her few cruisers on foreign service were a thorn in the side of the British Navy. It was not easy to reconcile the needs of the North Sea concentration with the duty of patrolling and protecting the tremendous length of sea routes along which supplies as well as troops were flowing from India and the Dominions to the support of the Mother Country. By the destruction of the *Emden* on November 9th, the Indian Ocean was finally cleared, but this success was offset by disaster in the Pacific, where Admiral Cradock's cruiser squadron was crushed by the heavier metal of Admiral von Spee's armoured cruisers, *Scharnhorst* and *Gneisenau*. This setback was, however, promptly redeemed by the Admiralty, who dispatched Admiral Sturdee with two battle cruisers, *Inflexible* and *Invincible*, on a lightning dash to the south Atlantic, while another battle cruiser, *Australia*, swept down from Fiji on Admiral von Spee's rear. Trapped on December 8th at the Falkland Isles, by this finely conceived surprise, Spee was sunk, and with him the last instrument of German naval power upon the oceans.

From this time onwards, the ocean communications of Britain and her Allies were secured for trade, for supplies and for the conveyance of troops. But as to all ocean routes there must be a land terminus, the development of the submarine made this security gradually less effective than it seemed on the morrow of Sturdee's victory.

The nature of the war at sea began to undergo definite changes early in 1915. During the first phase Britain had been too busy in clearing the seas and maintaining the security of the sea routes to devote much attention to the use of her sea command as an economic weapon against Germany. In any case her naval power was fettered by the artificial restrictions on blockade embodied in the Declaration of London of 1909, which the British Government with singular blindness announced on the outbreak of war that it would accept as the basis of maritime practice. Their release from these self-imposed fetters was aided by Germany's action.

On November 2nd, 1914, a German battle-cruiser squadron made a raid on the Norfolk coast, as a reconnaissance to test the scope of Britain's naval defence. Another followed on December 16th against the Yorkshire coast, Scarborough, Whitby and the Hartlepools being bombarded. Each time the Germans slipped away safely, but when they attempted a third, on January 24th, the English battle-cruiser squadron, under Beatty, trapped them off the Dogger Bank, sank the *Blücher* and badly damaged the *Derrfflinger* and *Seydlitz*. Although the stroke missed full success, it convinced the Germans of the futility of their attrition strategy, and Ingenohl, the commander of their High Seas Fleet, was replaced by Pohl, who proposed to Falkenhayn an offensive submarine campaign, which for success must be unlimited.

As a result, on February 18th, Germany proclaimed the waters round the British Isles a war zone where all ships, enemy or neutral, would be sunk at sight. This gave Britain a lever to loosen the Declaration of London, and she replied by claiming the right to intercept all ships suspected of carrying goods to Germany, and bring them into British ports for search. This tightening of the blockade caused serious difficulties with neutrals, America especially, but Germany eased the friction by torpedoing the great liner *Lusitania*, May 7th, 1915. The drowning of 1,100 people, including some Americans, was a spectacular brutality which shocked the conscience of the world, and appealed more forcibly to American opinion than even the desolation of Belgium. This act, succeeded by others, paved the way for the entry of the United States into the war, though it was to be later than seemed likely on the morrow of the tragedy.

One result of Britain's early established command of the sea was that it gave her the opportunity to sweep up Germany's oversea colonies with little hindrance or expenditure of force. Their seizure was valuable in that it gave the Allies important assets to bargain with in case of an unfavourable or negative issue to the war. At the end of August a New Zealand expedition captured Samoa, and in September an Australian expedition took possession of New Guinea; the Australian Navy also cleared several important German wireless stations in the Pacific Isles. Japan, entering the war on Britain's side, sent a division with a naval squadron, to besiege the German fortress of Tsing-tao on the coast of China. The first landing took place on September 2nd, and a tiny British contingent arrived on the 23rd, but the defences were modern, the land approach narrow, and the actual siege was not begun until October 31st. Seven days' bombardment was followed by an assault, which led to the capitulation of the garrison, after a rather feeble resistance.

In Africa, Togoland was occupied in August; the equatorial forest of the Cameroons was a sterner obstacle, and not until the beginning of 1916 were the German forces conquered by joint British and French forces after a prolonged but economically conducted campaign. General Botha, the South African Premier, once in arms against England, now for her, organized a force which conquered German South West Africa.

Almost concurrently Botha rendered a still greater service to the British cause by putting down the rebellion of a section of disaffected Boers, which, save for the Irish rising of Easter, 1916, was the only revolt within the borders of the Empire during these four trying years.

Only German East Africa, the largest and richest of Germany's colonies, remained, and that, owing to the difficulties of the country and the skill of General von Lettow-Vorbeck, the German commander, was not to be completely subdued until the end of 1917. An Expeditionary Force was sent thither in November to support the local British East African forces, and was repulsed at Tanga. To compensate his lack of troops, the German commander, Lettow-Vorbeck, found allies in the local bees, and his skilful tactics produced panic among the Indian battalions. Not until late in 1915 could the British Government, occupied with greater problems, spare either the time or the force to deal with this hornet's nest.

The year 1915 witnessed the dawn of another new form of war which helped to drive home the new reality that the war of armies had become the war of peoples. From January onwards, Zeppelin raids began on the English coast and reached their peak in the late summer of 1916, to be succeeded by aeroplane raids. The difficulty of distinguishing from the air between military and civil objectives smoothed the path for a development which, beginning with excuses, ended in a frank avowal that in a war for existence the will of the enemy nation, not merely the bodies of their soldiers, is the inevitable target. Although the Zeppelin raids in 1915 and 1916, through misdirection, did little material damage and caused less than two thousand casualties, it has been estimated that, by their disorganizing effect, about 'one sixth of the total normal output of munitions was entirely lost'.

The first psychological symptom of the World War, as it seemed to many, was an immeasurable sigh of relief. Had the peoples of Europe sat on the safety-valve too long? The war-weary mind of today cannot reconstruct the tension and anxiety, the strain and stress of hope and fear of the long years of the peace that was no peace and yet was not war. It may be read as a revolt of the spirit against the monotony and triviality of the everyday round, the completion of a psychological cycle when the memories of past wars have faded, and paved the way for the emergence and revival of the primordial 'hunting' instinct in man.

This first phase of enthusiasm was succeeded by one of passion, the natural ferocity of war accentuated by a form of mob spirit which is developed by a 'nation in arms'. The British Army was relatively immune because of its professional character, whereas in the German

Army, the most essentially 'citizen', it gained scope because of the cold-blooded logic of the general staff theory of war. With the coming of the autumn a third phase became manifest, more particularly among the combatants. This was a momentary growth of a spirit of tolerance, symbolized by the fraternization which took place on Christmas Day, but this in turn was to wane as the strain of the war became felt and the reality of the struggle for existence came home to the warring sides.

CHAPTER FOUR

SCENE 1

The Battle that was not, Yet Turned the Tide – the Marne

No battle has caused more controversy, produced so large a literature in so short a time, or given rise to more popular interest and legend than that of the Marne. But then this crisis of September, 1914, wrought the downfall of the German war plan and thereby changed the course of history. For if it be true, as it certainly is in part, that Germany lost the war when she lost this battle, it is natural that claimants to the distinction of having won it should be many.

The first legend to arise was that Foch had won it by driving the German centre into the marshes of St Gond, and even today, in total disregard of the facts and times of the battle, this is still given currency by reputable historians outside France.

But while, like a pebble dropped in water, the ripples of this story were still spreading, knowledgeable opinion in France was violently arguing whether the credit was due to Joffre, the Commander-in-Chief, or Galliéni, his quondam superior and then subordinate, who had delivered from Paris the blow at the German flank, exposed by Kluck's wheel inwards before Paris. One school contended that Joffre had conceived the idea of the counter-offensive, and at most admitted under pressure of facts that Galliéni's initiative in seeing the opportunity had given an impulse to Joffre's decision to seize it. The other school argued that Joffre, after the failure of his first attempt to stage a counter-offensive on the line of the Somme, had given up all idea of a fresh attempt at an early date, and that but for Galliéni's fiery determination and persuasion the retreat would have continued. A dispassionate judgement is now possible, and if we recognize that on Joffre fell the grave responsibility of taking the decision, the weight of evidence shows that Galliéni's inspiration dictated both the site and promptness of the thrust. Furthermore, it rebuts the alternative case of Joffre's advocates

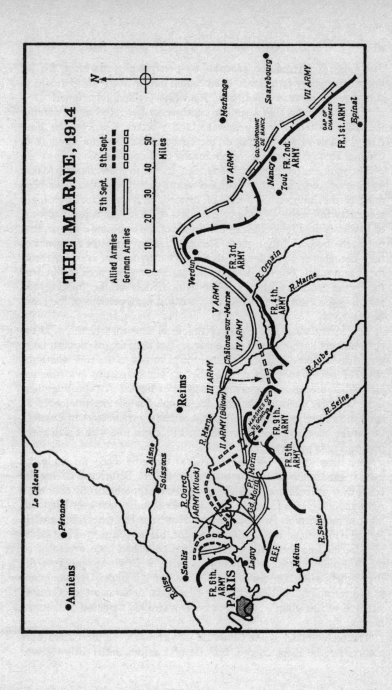

THE MARNE, 1914

Allied Armies
German Armies

5th Sept. 9th Sept.

Miles
0 10 20 30 40 50

Le Câteau
Péronne
Amiens
Soissons
R. Aisne
R. Oise
Senlis
Reims
FR. 6th. ARMY
PARIS
I ARMY (Kluck)
R. Ourcq
Lagny
B.E.F.
Gd. Pt. Morin
Pt. Morin
Melun
R. Seine
II ARMY (Bülow)
FR. 5th. ARMY
FR. 9th. ARMY
MARSHES OF ST GOND
R. Marne
III ARMY
Châlons-sur-Marne
IV ARMY
V ARMY
Verdun
FR. 3rd. ARMY
R. Ornain
FR. 4th. ARMY
R. Marne
R. Aube
R. Seine
VI ARMY
Gd. COURONNE DE NANCY
Nancy
Toul
FR. 2nd. ARMY
Morhange
Saarebourg
VII ARMY
GAP OF CHARMES
FR. 1st. ARMY
Epinal

that Galliéni marred the prospect by precipitating the blow, for we know that twenty-four hours' delay would have enabled the Germans to complete the protective redistribution which Galliéni interrupted.

On the German side a similar controversy has raged as to whether the order to retreat was a mistake, and whether Kluck of the First Army, Bülow of the Second, or the envoy of the Supreme Command, Colonel Hentsch, was responsible for the fatal decision.

The multiple controversy has at least served to show that the Marne was a psychological rather than a physical victory. So, also, have been most of the immortal victories of history, with the actual fighting a secondary influence. For the profoundest truth of war is that the issue of battles is usually decided in the minds of the opposing commanders, not in the bodies of their men. The best history would be a register of their thoughts and emotions, with a mere background of events to throw them into relief. But the delusion to the contrary has been fostered by the typical military history, filled with details of the fighting and assessing the cause of a victory by statistical computations of the number engaged.

The Marne was so clearly a psychological issue that the minds of the commanders have received due analysis. But even so, the 'combat complex' has tended to narrow the analysis of minds to the area where the clash of bodies took place. Thereby certain suggestive evidence has escaped comment. This evidence may be expressed in a startling question. Was the victory primarily due to the heated imagination of an English railway porter and to a party of temporary visitors to Ostend? Or, at the least, did these humble worthies constitute with Galliéni the mainspring of victory?

The suggestion is not so fantastic as it seems when we study the mental atmosphere of the German commanders. Before and during the crisis they were constantly looking backward apprehensively over their right shoulders, fearful of an Allied stroke against their ever-lengthening communications in Belgium and Northern France. Unfortunately for the Allies, there was small warrant for this nervousness. The belated plea for landing the BEF on the Belgian coast had been overruled by the Wilsonian pledge and policy of tying it as an appendix to the French left wing. Yet the Belgian Field Army, if under German guard at Antwerp, had at least caused a serious detachment of German strength to this guard – and more, was a chronic irritation to German nerves.

The fertile brain of Mr Churchill was also at work. Resources were scanty, but he dispatched a brigade of marines under Brig-General

Aston to Ostend, with orders to give their presence the fullest publicity. They landed on August 27th, and stayed ashore until the 31st.

Now to turn to the 'other side of the hill'. On September 5th, the day when the French troops were moving forward to strike at Kluck, Colonel Hentsch, the representative of the Supreme Command, came to the threatened army with this ominous and despairing warning – 'The news is bad. The Sixth and Seventh Armies are blocked. The Fourth and Fifth are meeting with strong resistance ... The English are disembarking fresh troops continuously on the Belgian coast. There are reports of a Russian expeditionary force in the same parts. A withdrawal is becoming inevitable.' We know from other sources that the 3,000 marines had grown in the German Command's imagination to 40,000, and that the Russians were said to be 80,000.

Thus the German flank army was left to face its ordeal with the belief that its rear was seriously menaced, and that in any case the Supreme Command was contemplating a withdrawal. At the least such knowledge must have been insidiously enervating during a period of strain. If the Supreme Command came to have doubts of the Belgian news, it also became imbued with the idea of a retirement, and when Hentsch came again on September 9th with full powers to coordinate it, 'should rearward movements have begun', not only had these begun, but they also coincided with fresh disturbing news from Belgium. For if the Belgian sortie from Antwerp that day was shortlived, it had all the incalculable psychological effect of menacing news at a moment of crisis. The German retreat gathered momentum and spread. With it turned the tide of the war.

History should do justice to Mr Churchill's happy inspiration and General Aston's handful of 'marine promenaders'. But equally helpful was that amazing 'Russian' myth which originated and spread so mysteriously. Mr Churchill, we know, had actually proposed to bring a Russian expeditionary force in such a way. Did the proposal perhaps leak out and become exaggerated into realization in the process? General opinion, however, has long ascribed the legend to the heated imagination of a railway porter working on the simple fact of the night passage of troop trains with Gaelic-speaking occupants. If so, a statue in Whitehall 'to the Unknown Porter' is overdue.

Keeping this external factor on the circumference of our thought, let us turn to trace the sequence of events in the actual battle zone. The immediate chain of causation begins with the escape by retreat of the French and British armies from the frontier trap into which Joffre's plan had led them. The first, highly coloured, reports from the army commands in the battles of the frontiers had given the German Supreme Command the impression of a decisive victory. It was under this hallucination that Moltke, on August 25th, cheerfully and needlessly dispatched four divisions to the Russian front – to the detriment of his right-wing punch, already weakened by seven divisions left for the investment of derelict fortresses – truly a bad investment. Then the comparatively small totals of prisoners raised doubts in Moltke's mind and led him to a more sober estimate of the situation. The Kaiser's easy optimism now irritated him – 'He has already a shout-hurrah mood that I hate like death.' The new pessimism of Moltke combined with the renewed optimism of his army commanders to produce a fresh change of plan, which contained the seeds of disaster.

While Kluck's army, on the German extreme right or outer flank, was pressing on the heels of the British – so close that the 'outside' British corps (Smith-Dorrien) was forced to halt and give battle – Kluck's neighbour on the inside, Bülow, was following up Lanrezac's French Fifth Army. When on August 26th the British left wing fell back southwards badly mauled from Le Cateau, Kluck had turned south-westwards again. If this direction was partly due to misconception of the line of retreat taken by the British – the idea that they were retreating to the Channel ports – it was also in accordance with his original role of a wide circling sweep. And by carrying him into the Amiens–Péronne area, where the first parts of the newly formed French Sixth Army were just detraining after their 'switch' from Alsace, it had the effect of dislocating Joffre's design for an early return to the offensive – by compelling the Sixth Army to fall back hurriedly towards the shelter of the Paris defences.

But Kluck had hardly swung out to the south-west before he was induced to swing in again. For in order to ease the pressure on the British, Joffre had ordered Lanrezac to halt and strike back against the pursuing Germans, and Bülow, shaken by the threat, called on Kluck for aid. Lanrezac's attack, on August 29th, was stopped before Bülow needed this help, but he asked Kluck to wheel in nevertheless, in order to cut off Lanrezac's retreat. Before acceding, Kluck referred to Moltke. The request came at a moment when Moltke was becoming perturbed in general over the way the French were slipping away from his embrace and, in particular, over a gap which had opened between his Second (Bülow) and Third (Hausen) Armies through the latter having already turned south, from south-west, to help the Fourth Army, its neighbour on the other flank. Hence Moltke approved Kluck's change of direction – which meant the inevitable abandonment of the original wide sweep round the far side of Paris. Now the flank of the wheeling German line would pass the near side of Paris and across the face of the Paris defences. By this contraction of his frontage for the sake of security Moltke sacrificed the wider prospects inherent in the wide circling sweep of the original plan. And, as it proved, instead of contracting the risk he exposed himself to a fatal counterstroke.

On the night of September 2nd Moltke sent a message to the right-wing commanders which confirmed the change of plan and fore-shadowed a new one. 'The French are to be forced away from Paris in a south-easterly direction. The First Army will follow in echelon behind the Second Army, and will be responsible henceforward for the flank protection of the force.' But the First Army was a full day's march ahead of the Second: if Kluck tried to carry out the second part of the message he would be neglecting the first part. Hence he decided to march on, while detailing an incomplete Reserve Corps and a depleted cavalry division to serve as a flank guard. How lightly he regarded any danger from Paris is also shown in the facts that no aircraft were allotted to the flank guard, and no air reconnaissance ordered to the westward.

Meantime Moltke was growing depressed and his decision to abandon the original plan was definitely taken on September 4th. In place of it, Moltke substituted a narrower envelopment, of the French centre and right. His own centre (Fourth and Fifth Armies) was to press south-east while his left (Sixth and Seventh Armies), striking south-westwards, sought to break through the fortified barrier between Toul and Epinal, the jaws thus closing inwards on either side of Verdun. Meantime his right (First and Second Armies) was to turn outwards and, facing west, hold off any countermove which the French might attempt from the neighbourhood of Paris. Moltke's order continued to ignore that Kluck was ahead of Bülow in the race southward and had already crossed the Marne. For it not only told Kluck to 'remain facing the east side of Paris' (ie facing west), but to remain north of the Marne while Bülow wheeled into line, facing west, between the Marne and the Seine. Thus to fulfil the order Kluck had not merely to halt, while Bülow caught up and passed him, but to perform a sort of backward somersault. Such gymnastics are somewhat upsetting to the equilibrium of a large army; and in this case the French countermove which Moltke wished to guard against had already begun before his new plan could take effect. More-over Kluck, reluctant to be thus deprived of the chance of being the agent of decisive victory, continued his advance south towards the Seine on the 5th, saying that 'the movement to face west might be made at leisure'. For the moment he still left the weak detachment of three brigades and a few cavalry to guard his flank. Next morning it was struck by the French Sixth Army moving out from Paris.

During these days the Franco-British retreat had continued. On August 30th, Joffre – yielding to the pressure of a Government alarmed at seeing him abandon the capital by his direction of retreat – detached Maunoury's Sixth Army to reinforce the Paris garrison. Parting with it signified his abandonment of the flank counterstroke, for this was the force he had assembled for its execution. Moreover, a memorandum drawn up that same day shows that he had transferred his faith to a counter-offensive against the German centre 'in the hope of accomplishing ... the rupture which we formerly attempted facing north-east and debouching from the Meuse'. On September 1st, Joffre issued orders for the retreat of the Allied armies to be continued to a line south of the Seine, Aube and Ornain rivers. Not only was the effect to take the armies away from and far to the south-east of Paris, but a commander who is contemplating an early counter-offensive does not place the obstacle of a river barrier between himself and the enemy. And a further note to the several army commanders next day added that it was Joffre's intention to 'organize and fortify' this line, whence he planned to deliver not an immediate but an eventual counter-offensive. That same day he replied to a suggestion of a stand on the Marne, made by Sir John French and communicated through the Minister of War:

I do not believe it possible to envisage a general action on the Marne with the whole of our forces. But I consider that the cooperation of the English Army in the defence of Paris is the only course that can give an advantageous result.

To the Minister of War and to Galliéni he repeated the same verdict. When zealous apologists say that the idea of a counter-offensive was at the *back* of Joffre's mind, the historian can agree. This array of evidence is more than sufficient to dispel the legend that Joffre had any intention of giving battle on the Marne or that he planned the counterstroke which tilted the balance so dramatically.

The definite nature of his reply was the more significant because, on September 1st, a staff officer with Lanrezac's army had found the German order for a change of direction in the wallet of a dead officer, and this was sent to Joffre's headquarters early next day. And on the morning of the 3rd, the changed direction, to the south-east, of Kluck's marching columns had been noticed and reported by British aviators. In the afternoon they added that these columns were crossing the Marne and in the evening Maunoury reported that there were no German troops left in the area west of the line Paris–Senlis. All this was reported to Joffre without making any impression on his plans – save that on the night of the 2nd he altered the limit of his retirement to a line still farther south!

But from Galliéni, the new military governor of Paris, even a fragment of information gained on the 3rd had drawn an instant response. He ordered Maunoury to carry out further air and cavalry reconnaissances as soon as it was light on the 4th. Quickly convinced by these early reports that the Germans were moving obliquely past the front of the Paris defences, exposing their own flank, Galliéni was equally quick to act. At 9 AM he ordered Maunoury's army to get ready for a move eastward to strike the Germans in flank. He then informed Joffre by telephone of his preparatory moves, and urged him to sanction a counter-offensive. (This consent was necessary not only to ensure a combined effort but because Joffre had persuaded the new Minister of War to subordinate Galliéni to himself.)

Galliéni's fiery and inspired arguments made an impression, but no more, on the slow-thinking Commander-in-Chief of the field armies. To save time while Joffre was still cogitating Galliéni rushed off by motor to Melun to explain the new situation to the British, and if possible gain their cooperation. Unfortunately, Sir John French was absent from his headquarters, and at first Galliéni could not even find Archibald Murray, his chief of the general staff. It was a curious scene. Galliéni, for his part, found the British staff unsettled and depressed, not hesitating to say that if England had known the condition of the French army she would not have entered the war. They were hardly in the mood to discern the underlying qualities of this most unmilitary-looking military genius, bespectacled and untidy, with shaggy moustache, black buttoned boots and yellow leggings. Little wonder perhaps that one eminent soldier with a pungent gift of humour remarked that 'no British officer would be seen speaking to such a — comedian'.

Galliéni pointed out to Murray that it was vital to seize the opportunity which the Germans had given by offering their right flank, told him that the 'Army of Paris' was already in motion against the German flank, and begged that the British should cease to retreat and join with his forces in an offensive next day. Murray, however, showed 'une grande répugnance ... à entrer dans nos vues', and declared that he could do nothing in the absence of his commander. After waiting three hours in vain for Sir John French's return, Galliéni had to leave at 5

PM with the mere promise of a telephone message later. This brought no satisfaction, for its purport was that the British would continue their retreat next day. Their decision had been confirmed by receiving a letter, written that morning, from Joffre who said: 'My intention, in the present situation, is to pursue the execution of the plan that I have had the honour to communicate to you – that of retiring behind the Seine – and only to engage on the selected line with all forces united.' The meagre influence which the news of Kluck's change of direction had achieved was shown by a subsequent paragraph which said: 'In the case of the German armies continuing their movement towards the SSE ... perhaps you will agree that your action can be most effectively applied on the right bank of the river, between the Marne and Seine.' This casual qualification to the definite opening statement gave the British little encouragement to fall in with Galliéni's audacious suggestion. There is a dramatic contrast between the sluggish working of Joffre's mind, gradually but all too slowly veering round, and Galliéni's swift *coup d'œil* and instantaneous reaction.

After Galliéni's morning message, Joffre had been moved so far as to send a telegram, timed 12.45 PM, to Franchet d'Esperey (who had superseded Lanrezac in command of the Fifth Army), saying – 'Please inform me if you consider that your army is in a state to make it [an attack] with any chance of success' – an inquiry which hardly suggests a sense of vital opportunity or an urge to action. This reached Franchet d'Esperey while Henry Wilson, of French's staff, was with him, and, after discussion, a reply was drafted, saying 'the battle cannot take place before the day after tomorrow', and that the Fifth Army would continue its retreat on the morrow, attacking on the 6th. To this message he added, in his own hand, a qualifying note even less encouraging: 'In order that the operation may be successful the necessary conditions are: (1) The close and absolute cooperation of the Sixth Army debouching on the left bank of the Ourcq on the morning of the 6th. It must reach the Ourcq tomorrow ... or the British won't budge. (2) My army can fight on the 6th, but its situation is not brilliant. No reliance can be placed on the reserve divisions.'

What was likely to be the effect on a Joffre of such a discouraging reply to his tentative inquiry? To harden his hesitation.

That hesitation was the more natural because Berthelot, his chief adviser, was vehemently in favour of continuing the retreat and maintaining the original plan. Then early in the afternoon came an ominous report of German progress across the Marne. As Joffre's own memoirs relate: 'This was all that was needed to cause Berthelot to return to the charge.' The memoirs, it is true, argue that Joffre merely continued to put off a decision, but they admit that he issued new instructions that were designed to accord with Berthelot's plan. Still more significantly, the decision was taken to move the headquarters over thirty miles farther south. Then, while Joffre was having an early dinner, Franchet d'Esperey's message arrived.

The next link in the chain of causation fits in with a click – the click of a telephone switch putting a call through. For if Galliéni's *coup d'œil* gained the opportunity it was, as he himself said, '*coups de téléphone* which gained the Battle of the Marne'. On returning to his headquarters in Paris he had found a belated message from Joffre which was favourable to his proposal for a counterstroke, but preferred it to be delivered south of the Marne – where it would have lost the greater effect given by a blow against the enemy's flanks and rear.

Galliéni seized the telephone, got through to Joffre, and by the fervour and force of his arguments at last won his sanction for the 'Army of Paris' to strike north of the Marne as part of a general counter-offensive by the left-wing armies. Joffre promised to obtain the co-operation of the British. Galliéni promptly issued orders (8.30 PM) to Maunoury's army, which he reinforced. After several hours' delay Joffre's orders were sent out for the offensive on September 6th – it was too late now for the 5th, and too late to be generally effective even for the 6th. The delay had far-reaching consequences – not all ill.

On the 5th while Maunoury's troops were moving east towards the enemy, both the British and Franchet d'Esperey's were marching south in accord with their original orders – away from the enemy, and even away from each other. But for Galliéni, the gap they thus opened might have proved perilous. When they turned about next day, they had much ground to recover, and were not as quick in retracing their steps as the situation demanded. This 'disappearance' of the British not only enabled but encouraged Kluck – who had been taken completely unawares – to pull back half his main body (II and IV Corps) from the sector where the British had been, to reinforce the hard-pressed flank guard which was trying to hold off Maunoury's menacing advance against the German rear. The arrival of these fresh forces began to check Maunoury's advance on the 7th, and Galliéni pushed forward every possible reserve he could scrape up in order to strengthen Maunoury.

Here occurred the famous if legend-crusted episode of the Paris taxi-cabs. A fresh division had just detrained near Paris, but it was forty miles from the battlefront. If it marched thither it would be too late, and there was only sufficient rail transport to take half the division.

That afternoon, the police held up taxicabs in the streets, bundling the passengers out in some cases, and, after collecting 600 cabs, sent them to the suburb of Gagny where they filled up with soldiers. Galliéni came to see the performance and, with mingled gratification and amusement, exclaimed: 'Well, at least it's not commonplace!' During the night this forerunner of the future motorized column swept, as only Paris taxicabs can sweep, through the outlying villages and past their amazed inhabitants, making two journeys, with 3,000 soldiers at a time. Unfortunately these taxicabs maintained their traditional preference for speed over reliability and, passing and repassing, became so mixed that on the morning of the 8th several hours were spent in sorting out their passengers before the division could attack.

The pressure on the Germans gained extra force from the fact that it was directed against their rear flank. If Galliéni had received the two further army corps for which he had asked days before and which were only just arriving piecemeal, the German forces south of the Marne might have been cut off and the battle been as decisive tactically as it was strategically. Even in the actual situation, the menace was such that at 10 PM on the 6th Kluck called back his two remaining army corps, so creating a thirty-mile-wide gap between himself and the neighbouring army of Bülow. Only two weak cavalry corps, with a few Jäger battalions, were left to fill it and Kluck failed to arrange that this thin screen should be put under a single command. The consequences were fatal. Although he was able to hold and even press back Maunoury's troops, the gap he had left in the southern front uncovered Bülow's flank. Although still untouched by Franchet d'Esperey's slow advance on the 7th, Bülow, sensitive to his raw side, drew back his right to the north bank of the Petit Morin. And when news came that the British were advancing into the centre of the gap, it proved the signal for the German retreat, which began on September 9th. If the continuance of the British withdrawal on September 5th had marred the chance of a crushing victory, it was a pleasant irony of fate that their very withdrawal made possible the 'victory' as actually achieved.

It is necessary, however, to take account of the situation on other parts of the battlefront for, unless the German intentions elsewhere had been frustrated, Joffre's victory would have been impossible and defeat probable. To the frustration of their left wing attack in the east, or Lorraine sector, the Germans themselves were the chief contributors; for by pressing the French back on their own fortress line they had already made their task of breaking through it almost impossible. And yet another of the many 'accidents of the Marne' made their repulse

THE BATTLE OF THE MARNE

certain; for when Dubail's and de Castelnau's armies, after their defeat in the battle of Morhange–Sarrebourg, ended their hasty retreat, their line sagged inwards; and into this re-entrant, formed quite unintentionally, the main German attack was launched, pushing towards that very 'gap of Charmes' which the French in earlier years had prepared for their reception.

Thus the French were given an opportunity to strike back effectively at the Geman flanks, and thereby they temporarily paralysed the original German advance, which came to a halt on August 27th. This not only gave the French breathing space to strengthen their position, but enabled Joffre, with safety, to transfer part of the force from the right wing to the more critical left wing. News of this transfer inspired Moltke to frame his new plan of September 5th, and lured him into another vain attack on the French fortified barrier, despite protest from the Crown Prince Rupprecht of Bavaria, commanding the Sixth Army. The new attack was launched frontally against the Grand Couronné de Nancy, the ridge which formed a flank buttress for the gap of Charmes. And the Kaiser arrived with his white cuirassiers, like an actor waiting his call, to make a triumphal entry into Nancy. But successive assaults, inadequately prepared, collapsed under the well-knit and superior fire of the French artillery, and on September 8th Moltke ordered Rupprecht to stop the offensive and the vain loss of life. Rupprecht had been urged into it against his own judgement by the excessive confidence of the artillery expert, Major Bauer, that his super-heavy howitzers would have the same effect as on the obsolete Belgian fortresses. Yet, curiously, he now only gave up the attack under protest – so Micawberish was the judgement of the military leaders of 1914–18.

The German centre (Fifth and Fourth Armies), west of Verdun, was no better able to fulfil its role as the right arm of the pincer-like squeeze ordained in Moltke's modified plan. In the Verdun area Sarrail had replaced Ruffey as commander of the French Third Army, and the first instructions he received indicated not only a continued retreat but the abandonment of Verdun. Sarrail thought differently, however, and determined to cling on to the Verdun pivot as long as possible, without losing touch with the Fourth Army to the west. It was a happy piece of initiative, and the brake thus placed on the south-eastward advance of the enemy's Fifth Army (under the German Crown Prince) was an essential factor in upsetting Moltke's plan. The stout resistance of Sarrail's troops, and still more the deadly fire of their artillery, not only held up but paralysed the Crown Prince's advance. And a belated attempt on the 9th to break the deadlock by a night attack, ended in a suicidal fiasco, with the Germans firing on each other. Sarrail, however, asked in vain for reinforcements which might have enabled him to convert his resistance into a dangerous counterstroke from Verdun westwards against the German flank – for by holding on to Verdun he had formed one side of a sack into which the German armies between him and Maunoury, on the other side, had pushed.

The German Third Army (Hausen) formed a link between the German centre and right wing, and was assigned the indefinite role of being ready to support either. This role was perhaps in part the reflection of the fact that, being composed of Saxons, the Prussians tended to discount its value. In the event it was virtually divided. Its left was used to help the Fourth Army in the abortive attack on the French Fourth Army (de Langle de Cary); an attack which, after perhaps the severest fighting of the whole battle, was driven to ground by the French artillery. Its right joined with Bülow's left in an attack on Foch, who had taken over command of a new Ninth Army, in the French centre, formed by simple subtraction from de Langle de Cary's army.

Among all the legends of the Marne that which has grown up round Foch's part is the most comprehensive and has the least substance. The first claim, still widely believed, is that Foch decided the issue of the whole battle by a counterstroke which threw the Prussian Guard 'into the marshes of St Gond'. In fact, however, the Germans took their leave without interference – after the issue had been decided farther west. The second, and more modest claim, is that Foch made the victory possible by preventing a German breakthrough in the French centre. Even this is inaccurate – because the Germans were not trying to break through here. Bülow was merely carrying out his new protective task of wheeling his line to face west. And, in the course of this wheel, his left wing naturally bumped against Foch's front.

A further paradox is that although Foch issued repeated orders for attacks, his troops in reality were on the defensive, a defence needlessly desperate owing to his own disobedience of orders.

At 1.30 AM on September 6th, Foch had received Joffre's famous order for the general 'about turn'. Unlike the other armies, he received it in time to act on his share of it, which was to cover the flank of Franchet d'Esperey's attack by holding the southern exits of the marshes of St Gond. Instead, he concentrated the bulk of his forces for an offensive north of the marshes, leaving the weak XI Corps to hold the wide and vulnerable sector east of the marshes. His troops were tired and much reduced by the hard retreat, and their offensive quickly died away; in their reflux they failed to hold firmly the southern exits of the marshes. Thus Foch continued to keep his main strength on that flank. But the Germans could only cross by the narrow causeways, and in consequence made a side-step – as they might have done earlier. On the 7th, their attack east of the marshes broke down under the fire of the French artillery. As the only way of evading it, a bayonet attack in the half-light before dawn was arranged. This caught Foch's right by surprise and it gave way rapidly. Fortunately the Germans did not follow up as rapidly and so captured few of the tormenting guns. Even so, the situation was serious and Foch called for help; Franchet d'Esperey lent a corps to support his left and Joffre sent another to fill the gap now yawning on his right. On the 9th the continued German attack against Foch's right made fresh progress and met little resistance – until, shortly before 2 PM, it was stopped by receiving Bülow's now notorious order for a general retirement. The Germans drew off undisturbed and even unobserved. To meet the earlier emergency Foch had taken the 42nd Division from his intact left wing and switched it across to his right; but it only arrived in time to fire its guns in the twilight after the vanished foe – contrary to the popular legend of its decisive counterstroke against the flank of the German breakthrough. And one has to add that although Bülow had exposed his flank in making the wheel, Foch thought only of making a frontal counterattack. On the battle as a whole his main, and most serious, effect was that he detracted from the main offensive instead of helping to cover it.

In our survey of the battlefront we have now travelled back to the decisive western flank. Let us focus our eyes on the various headquarters behind the German front and examine the wavering gusts of opinion which culminated in the German retirement. The Supreme Command was back at Luxembourg, whither it had moved from Coblenz, on August 30th, and depended for communication with the armies on wireless, supplemented by occasional visits by staff officers in motor-cars. No regular motor or motorcycle dispatch service had been organized, and wireless communication suffered not only from the time lost in enciphering and deciphering but from interference from the Eiffel Tower in Paris. As the army commanders, faithful to the tradition of 1870, were jealous of control, information was as sparse as it was slow except when they had successes to report – and exaggerate. Throughout the crisis of the battle, from September 7th–9th, no single report of any value came back from the front and, as late as the 12th, Moltke had no knowledge of what had happened to Kluck's army, or where it was. Perhaps this ignorance made little difference, for on the

5th, Falkenhayn, then at Luxembourg in his capacity of Minister of War, noted in his diary: 'Only one thing is certain: our General Staff has completely lost its head. Schlieffen's notes do not help any further, and so Moltke's wits come to an end.'

Moreover, Moltke had already reconciled himself to defeat. For the gloom at Luxembourg is well shown by the fact that when, on September 8th, Lieut-Colonel Hentsch left, as his emissary, to visit in turn the five armies west of Verdun, he was given full powers to coordinate the retreat, 'should rearward movements have been initiated'. He found none had occurred, if he found little confidence, at the headquarters of the Fifth, Fourth, and Third Armies. Passing on he spent the night of the 8th with Bülow, and there found such an intensification of gloom that when he left in the morning he could at least feel confidence on one point – that orders for a retreat would soon be given. And about 9 AM on the 9th air reports told Bülow that six enemy columns (five British and one of French cavalry) were approaching the Marne – and so entering the mouth of the gap. By 11 AM he had issued orders for the retreat of his army to begin at 1 PM, sending word to Kluck of his action.

Hentsch, delayed by blocks and panics on the road, did not reach Kluck's headquarters till almost noon. There, according to his evidence, he found that orders for a retirement had already gone out, and in confirming them merely added the direction of the retreat – northeastward. But Kluck's Chief of Staff, Kuhl, asserts that these orders were only the mistake of a subordinate and that he had merely ordered a swing-back of his left in view of the fact that the British were almost behind it. He further says that Hentsch, in view of Bülow's situation, gave him orders to retreat. And Hentsch is not alive to contradict him. But the facts that the withdrawal began at 2 PM, that the roads behind had been cleared, and that neither Kuhl nor Kluck troubled to ask for a written order, go far to support Hentsch – by showing their eagerness to be off. Kuhl, indeed, has admitted that the imminent breakthrough of the British and Franchet d'Esperey made the retreat inevitable. And, owing to the British penetration, Kluck's army had to retreat northward, thus leaving the gap still open.

The most curious of all the many accidents of the Marne is its accidental reproduction of the perfect pattern Napoleonic battle – the pattern which Napoleon several times fulfilled and which General Camon and other students believe was normally in his mind. Its characteristics were that while the enemy was gripped in front, a manoeuvre was directed against one of his flanks, a manoeuvre which was intended not to be decisive in itself but to create the opportunity for a decisive stroke. For the threat of envelopment caused a stretching of the enemy's line to ward it off and so created a weak joint on which the decisive stroke then fell. On the Marne Galliéni caused this stretching and the British pierced the joint. The pattern was executed perfectly, yet quite unconsciously.

Hence we see clearly that the continued retreat of the British on the 5th and their slow advance on the 6th and 7th were strategically invaluable, holding back unintentionally as Napoleon would have done purposely. If their 'decisive' thrust had been disclosed earlier, the joint would hardly have been weakened by the removal of Kluck's last two corps – the departure of which, even as it was, Bülow delayed until early on the 8th. And the fact that Maunoury's stroke was definitely checked while these two corps were still on the march towards him is sufficient evidence that his stroke in itself could not have caused a decision.

But the continued slowness of the advance on the 8th, 9th and 10th was the negation of the Napoleonic pattern. And it proved fatal to the chance of converting the German retreat into a disaster. Thereby it paved the way for the four long years of trench warfare. In part it was due to the obstacle provided by successive rivers. But in still greater part it was due to want of impulsion, and misguided direction. Sir John French seems to have had little faith in the prospect, and still less in his Allies' efforts. In consequence he trod on the brake rather than the accelerator, besides keeping most of his cavalry on his right flank, and even in rear of it, as a link with his French neighbour instead of a spearhead of the pursuit.* Indeed, not until the 11th was the cavalry really launched in pursuit. Franchet d'Esperey's advance was even more

---

* The average advance on the 6th was eleven miles; on the 7th, less than eight miles; on the 8th, ten miles; on the 9th, seven miles. The Official History argues that, under the conditions, 'little more could be expected'. This view does not agree with the evidence of numerous officers who took part. Thus General Charteris has a diary note, referring to the 7th – 'Actually, our own troops, though the men were very keen, moved absurdly slowly ... The cavalry were the worst of all, for they were right behind the infantry.' He also says that Haig went 'from one Divisional HQ to another trying to urge them forward', but the divisional diaries imply the opposite; it is certain that on the 9th Haig imposed a halt of several hours after crossing the Marne until his aircraft reported 'all clear'. He was then stopped again by French. The slowness of the advance is ascribed by General Gough to the fact that 'no attempt was made by GHQ to explain to the corps and divisional commanders the extraordinary opportunity now available for a decisive blow at the enemy'.

cautious: his right was tied back to Foch; his centre slowly followed up, but did not catch up, Bülow's retiring wing; his left neglected to push along a completely open path.

A further cause of delay, however, was the tactical method employed in the advance. The old idea of keeping an even alignment still ruled, as it did until 1918, so that if one corps or division was checked its neighbours tended to halt. Thus frequent opportunities were missed for pushing on past the flanks of a temporary resistance and maintaining the momentum of the advance. And because the British and French missed this opportunity it was to be left for 1918 to see and the Germans to apply the method of Nature – for thus does any current or stream take the line of least resistance, finding a way past an obstacle and then flowing on, while the back eddies wash away the now isolated obstacle.

Perchance also the victory might have been more decisive – to the shortening of the war – if its creator had not been removed from control at the beginning of it. Having already limited the power of Galliéni's blow, Joffre seized the first chance to deprive him of his powers of directing it. Would that he had been as quick in exploiting the weakness of the rival army! For on September 11th Joffre informed Galliéni that he would resume direct control of Maunoury's army, leaving Galliéni to fret his soul within the confines of Paris while watching the fruits of victory slipping from the grasp of his slow-thinking superior. Throughout the battle Galliéni's governing idea had been to direct all reserves to the north – towards the enemy's rear – although several times frustrated by Joffre. With Galliéni's disappearance the advance became purely frontal, giving the Germans the breathing space to reorganize and stand firm on the line of the Aisne. Not until then, September 17th, did Joffre's mind awake to the idea of concentrating by rail a fresh mass of manoeuvre behind the German flank. As a result, in the so-called 'Race to the Sea', the French were always 'an army corps too few and twenty-four hours too late', until the trench front stretched to the sea.

But his was not the sole failure to take advantage of the temporary state of disorder and indecision behind the German line. It is the sober verdict of General Edmonds, the British official historian, that – 'Had some of the fourteen British Territorial Force divisions and fourteen mounted brigades, with the 6th Division still in England, been landed at the Channel coast ports to fall on the German communications and rear, a decisive tactical result might have been obtained and the war finished.'

Even as it was, on reaching the Aisne an opportunity had remained, only to be missed. Indeed, the Official History states that 'The prospects of a breakthrough never were brighter' than on the morning of the 13th. Thanks to German carelessness and the initiative of various junior commanders, the passage of the river had been achieved on both flanks. And 'from all the information furnished to General Haig the gap had not been closed which had existed between the German First and Second Armies ever since the Battle of the Marne...' But the race was lost owing to 'a failure of the High Command to appreciate the situation'. On the 13th 'the divisions made a rather cautious and leisurely advance', and 'in the GHQ orders there was no hint whatever of the importance of time'.

'By the evening of the 13th September the situation had completely changed. German reinforcements were known to have arrived, and serious resistance was to be expected on the 14th; yet the GHQ orders merely repeated the formula that "the Army will continue the pursuit".' 'There was no plan, no objective, no arrangements for cooperation, and the divisions blundered into battle.' With their failure, the flux crystallized and deadlock ensued.

A still greater opportunity was thrown away by the French to the eastward; for, on reaching the Aisne, Conneau's cavalry corps and a group of reserve divisions were opposite a ten-mile gap in the German front. After crossing the river the cavalry rode on thirteen miles northwards to Sissonne – but then, 'seeing the danger' of being cut off, 'the order was given to retire to the bridges'. This inglorious sense of precaution forfeited an opening such as cavalry would never again enjoy on the Western Front. For, at Sissonne, Conneau's cavalry corps was fifteen miles north of the thrown-back flank of the German Second Army, and forty miles behind the line of the Third Army. 'It had only to move eastwards across the enemy lines of communication to cause at least alarm and confusion.'

The question has often been posed whether the trench stalemate would have come to pass if France had possessed a Napoleon. Although the unappreciated defensive power of modern weapons and the unwieldy masses of 1914 weighted the scales against the mobility and decisiveness of warfare, the Galliéni interlude raises a doubt. For not only did Galliéni afford the one instance of 'Napoleonic *coup d'œil*' witnessed on the Western Front in 1914–18, but his intuition, his boldness of manoeuvre and his swift decision were so vivid a contrast to that of the other leaders, French, British and German, as to suggest that it was possible to snatch a decision by manoeuvre from the jaws of trench warfare – before the artizan swallowed the artist.

The hypothesis is strengthened by the fact that Galliéni's influence was exercised under the most shackling conditions. The command of a fortress was governed by rules and limitations which ordained a strictly defensive role, even gave the governor power to refuse assistance to the field armies, and discouraged him from any wider horizon than that of his immediate responsibility for the defence of the fortress. It was the irony of fortune that the Commander-in-Chief in the field should have led the way to universal siege warfare; that the commander of a fortress should have conceived and launched the most decisive manoeuvre of the war. Yet war is a game where the 'joker' counts, and when Joffre withheld the trump Galliéni played the 'joker'. As he remarked later, half humorously, half bitterly, 'There has not been a battle of the Marne. Joffre's instructions ordained a retreat on the Seine and the evacuation of Verdun and of Nancy. Sarrail did not obey: he saved Verdun; Castelnau held on to the Grand Couronné: he saved Nancy. I have taken the offensive. As for asserting now that it is the Commander-in-Chief – who had gone back far to the rear while I advanced – who conducted, foresaw, and arranged it all ... it is hard to believe!'

The truest phrase of all was his first – 'There has not been a Battle of the Marne.' Nor had there been a 'battle' of Sedan in 1870. The folly of MacMahon in face of the first Moltke was paralleled, and even excelled, by the folly of the second Moltke in face of shadows.

CHAPTER FOUR

SCENE 2

The Field of Legend – Tannenberg

Like that of the Marne, the popular story of the great German victory of Tannenberg is a monument of monumental error. For it consists, actually, of a figure of wood, on a pedestal of clay, varnished with legend.

The first and most popular of these legends provided a romantic picture of an old general who, as the hobby of his years of retirement, spent his time in devising a gigantic trap for a future Russian invasion, exploring paths through and sounding the bottom of the marshes in which the Russian hordes were to be engulfed – and then, when war came, carrying his dream to fulfilment. The next legend, which rose as the shadow of Ludendorff rose behind the figure of Hindenburg, was of a masterly plan for a second Cannae conceived and dictated in the train that was carrying Ludendorff to pick up his nominal master *en route* to East Prussia. History, alas, must dissipate both.

For the Germans, essentially a people of combination, found their Galliéni in a conjunction between the brain of a young staff officer and the drive of an old corps commander. And they, in turn, were much helped because Russian leadership was able to combine the faults of a Moltke and a Joffre. Indeed, the military history of modern Russia is epitomized in the brief record of the invasion of East Prussia.

The man who was, in large measure, responsible for the blundering execution was also responsible for that disastrous invasion being made, and being made before the Russian forces were ready. This was General Jilinsky, who had been Chief of the General Staff until 1913. For he had made the military convention with France whereby Russia was pledged to put 800,000 men in the field on the fifteenth day of mobilization. This arrangement put a strain on the cumbrous Russian war machine which caused numerous cracks and local failures when it began moving. And it also put a strain on the Russian Headquarter staff which

TANNENBERG 1914

Baltic Sea

Situation on Aug. 27th.
VI ⇦ Russian Corps
XX ◂■ German Corps
→ Subsequent German movements
+++ Railway

N

Königsberg

XX Insterburg
Gumbinnen

III
IV

FIRST ARMY (Rennenkampf)

Mulhausen

East Prussia

Lautern
Bossau

½ II ½ II
Lötzen

MASURIAN LAKES

Allenstein
Osterode
XIII

I R XVII
VI

Deutsch Eylau

Hohenstein
XV
Tannenberg
XXII
Frogenau
XX
Lahna
Neidenburg   Willenburg

Ortelsburg

RUSSIA

I
Usdau
Soldau

SECOND ARMY (Samsonov)

Frontier

Mlawa

Ostrolenka

0 10 20 30 40
Miles

led them to make decisions in a state of nervous flurry. But the arrangement did not end with this promise, for the new plan envisaged an offensive against the Germans simultaneously with the main thrust against the Austrians.

To increase the drawbacks the plan was to be carried out by a man who had not worked it out; who had even been deprived deliberately of any influence upon it by General Sukhomlinov, the Minister of War. Sukhomlinov, indeed, was scheming to get command himself. But he was not the only one who had a belief in his own divine fitness for command. And his rival claimed divine right. For when the war came the Tsar proposed to take command himself – to the alarm of his ministers. Under pressure from them the Tsar regretfully appointed the Grand Duke Nicholas, who was at least a trained soldier, but handicapped him by nominating his two principal assistants. One of these, Yanushkevich, was a courtier general, unpopular with the working army. The second, Danilov, was an able but orthodox soldier, and really directed the Russian strategy.

From the earliest days of August the Grand Duke was incessantly pressed by the French, through the Russian Foreign Office, to do something to relieve the German pressure on the French, and to do it quickly. Thereby, although the Russian invasion of East Prussia did not begin before the promised time it began before it was ready.

East Prussia formed a long tongue of land pointing across the Niemen river, to the heart of Russia, and flanked on the north by the Baltic and on the south by Russian Poland. Along the land frontier two armies had been assembled, the First or Vilna Army under Rennenkampf and the Second or Warsaw Army under Samsonov. The two formed a group under the higher control of Jilinsky. His plan was that Rennenkampf should advance against the eastern tip of East Prussia, drawing upon himself the German defending forces; then, two days later, Samsonov was to cross the southern frontier and bestride the Germans' rear, cutting them off from the Vistula. The fault of this plan lay not in the conception but in the execution. Its potential value was well proved by the alarm – indeed, the dislocation of mind – caused in the German headquarters when the menace was disclosed. But it suffered two natural handicaps, apart from faulty leadership and military unreadiness. The first was that the two armies were separated by the fifty-mile chain of the Masurian Lakes; these also, in conjunction with the fortified Königsberg area on the west, narrowed Rennenkampf's line of advance to a gap only about forty miles wide. Secondly, the Russians' own invasion from the south was now to be handicapped by the fact that they had left the border country a desert, with poor railways and worse roads, as a barrier against a German invasion.

On August 17th, Rennenkampf crossed the eastern frontier with six and a half divisions and five cavalry divisions. The problem of meeting such a double thrust had long been studied, and Schlieffen's solution had been that of utilizing the obstacles of the county, especially the Masurian Lakes, to strike hard and with full strength at whichever Russian army first came within reach, and then to turn against the other. But Prittwitz, the commander in East Prussia, was akin to his superior, Moltke, in his fear of taking calculated risks. Unwilling to rely on Landwehr and garrison troops to supplement natural obstacles in delaying Samsonov, he also left the two divisions of the XX Corps (Scholtz) on the southern front. The remainder of his Eighth Army, seven divisions and one cavalry division, concentrated to oppose Rennenkampf. And, to handicap himself further in gaining quick and decisive results, he launched a frontal attack on the invaders - owing to a mistaken idea of their position.

This attack was delivered near Gumbinnen on August 20th. The German centre corps, the XVII (Mackensen), had to deliver the most straightforward attack and suffered a heavy repulse, which offset - at least psychologically - the success of the corps on either wing. Even so, Rennenkampf was on the point of ordering a retreat to save his own centre from encirclement when, next morning, he found that the Germans were retreating instead.

For on the day of Gumbinnen Samsonov had reached the frontier, so hurried on by Jilinsky, that his troops were tired and hungry, their transport incomplete and the supply services in chaos. He had with him eight divisions and three cavalry divisions, while two more divisions were following on.

His appearance was reported by the XX Corps to Prittwitz, and his force was rather under than over estimated. Prittwitz was unnerved by the news, although the XX Corps was not. That evening two of his staff, General Grünert and Lieut-Colonel Max Hoffmann were talking outside their office in the headquarters at Neidenburg - uncomfortably close to the southern frontier - when Prittwitz appeared and called them into his office. There also was the Chief of Staff, Count Waldersee, another wavering bearer of a famous name. With anxiety writ on his face, Prittwitz said - 'I suppose, gentlemen, you also have received this fresh news from the southern front? The army is breaking off the battle and retiring behind the Vistula.'

Both the junior staff officers protested, urging that the Gumbinnen